GOING HOME AGAIN

LOUISE HANNAH

ARPress
ILLUMINATING IDEAS
EMPOWERING VOICES

ARPress
45 Dan Road Suite 36
Canton MA 02021

Hotline: 1(800) 220-7660
Fax: 1(855) 752-6001

Ordering Information:
Quantity Sales. Special discounts are available on quantity purchases by corporations, associations, and others. For details, contact the publisher at the address above.

Printed in the United States of America.

ISBN-13   Paperback   979-8-89389-622-0
               eBook   979-8-89389-623-7

Library of Congress Control Number: 2024921318

Louise
Going Home Again

Growing up in Miami, Florida in the sixties was truly a time of confusion for me. It was also a time when the US was at war with Viet-Nam, mad with Cuba, and we were a class and a race-divided nation. I experienced the lost of friends that went off to war. I experienced segregation, and integration. I even experienced immigration during my high school years. Added to all of that were the unfair commands of my Daddy's Rules.

The sixties was a time when I was trying to find my own little "nitch," my own place in the world around me. But Daddy's Rules offered no comfort or kindness, especially if they were disobeyed. Daddy was the kind of man whose commands could not be taken lightly.

Teen pregnancy was on the rise during that time. My older sister, Anne, was one of its victims. It was because of her that Daddy added more amendments to his House Rules. I thought they were cruel, unfair, and I hated them. In my desire to escape Daddy's Rules and find myself, I left home as a teen.

The most exposure to the outside world, I had had was at school when the other kids talked about what was going on. It was at school where I heard my classmates and teachers talk about Martin Luther King Jr. and his movement. I learned just enough to make me dream of being free to go anywhere I wanted to go.

But Daddy said that things were the way they were, and it was never going to change—just more of us were going to be killed. "Don't put your hopes in all of that because you'll only be disappointed," Daddy would say. Later in high school I learned of the Black Panthers.

But I wasn't even allowed to say "Black Panthers" in our house because Daddy would have a "Conniption." (That's a word we'd used when someone was out of control; it was worse than having a fit.)

When I met Jay he told me all about the Black Panthers and their movement. The things Jay taught me about the Panthers gave me hope again: hope that who I was mattered, and hope that I was somebody. In my own home, I was always reminded that I was black, that I was a girl, and that I was not yet grown. I would soon be going out into the real world, and my self-esteem was on a down-hill slide.

Although this book is based on a true story, I have changed the names of the characters. I also changed the fate of a couple of characters.

ᏟᏅᏓᏅᏟᏆᏟᏅᏓ

This book is dedicated to GOD who inspired me to write it and for keeping me until I finished it.

I want to thank my sister Clara and her son Brandon for supplying me with the tools I needed. They brought me into the 21st century by buying me a laptop computer to use and taught me how to use it.

I want to thank my sister Karen and my daughters for their encouragement. Thanks also to my son Robert and his wife Brejo for taking time to help bring this book to life.

I want to give a special thanks to Phyllis Porter Dolislager for putting it all together for me.

ᏟᏅᏓᏅᏟᏆᏟᏅᏓ

Table of Contents

CHAPTER 1

December 1971

J ay bought a one-way airline ticket for Vanessa and me to Miami, Florida. During our ride to the airport, Jay and Diamond Jim talked about how the business was doing at The Club. All the while my little Vanessa and I sat in the back seat, not very happy about going to Miami. And the last year of my life in Detroit kept playing itself out in my head.

The last time I had gone to an airport, I was leaving Miami. Running away to be with Jay, the man I loved. Now I'd be showing up a year later, with a broken spirit, a baby in my arms, one on the way, and minus the husband I had left behind. Maybe once I forgive myself, my family will forgive me for leaving the way I did. I had been seventeen, and I thought that I knew what I wanted, and where I was going. But all I really knew was that I was the third oldest of five siblings, two older and two younger, and parents that set strong rules for us, some of which were very unfair. The rules were:

Love God

Love each other

Make good grades and get a good education Stay in the house: learn to cook, clean, and sew

Don't ask questions, follow the rules, Daddy knows what's best No parties or phone calls, in or out, until you're 16

No after school activities

Don't get married or have sex until you're forty

I remember when I was thirteen; I was really good at volleyball. I was one of the best in our area, and my Phys. Ed. teacher talked me into staying after school to play in a championship game. I told my teacher that I had not asked my daddy, but she said that she'd talk to Daddy because the game was a school project. I said, OK, and I stayed. My school was winning the game; my teammate was getting ready to set the ball up so that I could spike the ball across the net. After everyone took their places, I looked out across the baseball field, and I could see Daddy coming toward the court. He had taken his belt off and had it in his hand. I knew that I was going to get it.

When the ball was set up for me, instead of spiking the ball across the net, I ran as fast as I could to meet Daddy on the baseball diamond, before he got to the court where we were having the Championship Game. When I got to Daddy, I told him that my teacher said that she was going to talk to him. But Daddy just reminded me of his rules and told me to go to the car, but not to run. I could feel Daddy's belt as it lashed across my back, my side, my head, arms and legs. I could also hear the laughter coming from the volleyball courts. I just wanted to crawl home, underground, die, and never go back to school, ever again.

After that day the kids teased me all the time. But Mrs. Graham, my Phys. Ed teacher would punish the kids whenever she'd see them teasing me; sometimes she even sent them to the Principal's office. But she never talked to Daddy about what happened. And I never disobeyed Daddy's Rules again.

We are at the airport now. We check our bags. I give Vanessa to Jay to hold because I know that it will be awhile before she'll be in his arms again. I guess we'd better get all of our hugs and kisses now. Jay and I kiss and agree to contact each other every week by phone or letter.

We arrived at Miami International Airport in about four hours. The plane landed, and it was time to get off. I collected all of my things and put them into one bag, so that I could carry the bag on one arm and Vanessa on the other. I finally managed to walk down the small aisle, turning sideways so I didn't bang Vanessa against the seats. As I walked from the plane to the terminal lobby, it felt as though I had about fifty pounds in my arms.

After we got into the lobby I started to look around for Daddy. He said that he'd pick me up, but there was no trace of him. Just as I was about to sit down with Vanessa, I saw my sister Bobbie hurrying across the floor to greet me. She gave me a big hug and a peck on the cheek. She took Vanessa right out of my arms. She was kissing Vanessa, hugging her and talking to her. Bobbie completely forgot about me, and some strange looking guy was standing behind her. The more I looked at him, it came to me that this was the guy that she had described to me on the phone. This was the guy that she was going to marry soon. He had straight black hair, olive skin, dark lips and a pleasing smile. We both looked at Bobbie while she was getting acquainted with Vanessa. I cleared my throat to get her attention. After Bobbie got her composure, she introduced us to each other.

"Louise, I'd like you to meet Freddy." "Freddy this is my sister Louise."

Freddy was from Trinidad; his family was still there. He was an exchange student, living in the U.S. on a visa until he finished school. Bobbie said that they used to see each other at the library at school, at least three times a week. That is how they met each other. Then they started talking to each other, and then Freddy started asking her out on dates. After that she knew he was the one.

Freddy and I shook hands and said hello. There wasn't too much for us to talk about because we really didn't know each other. We all walked to the baggage claim area. I walked behind them as they played with Vanessa. They looked like a little family. I wished that Jay had come home with me to meet the folks as a family.

While we waited for my bags to come around on the carousel, I began to feel sick again, like I wanted to throw up right there. So I excused myself and went to the bathroom. When I got into the stall, I threw up everything that they had given me on the plane. (In the 70's, airlines served complete meals to everyone.) I was feeling very nauseous and shaky. When I came out of the stall, I rinsed my mouth and then found some saltine crackers in my purse to settle my stomach before I went back out to get my luggage.

When I got back to the carousel, Bobbie and Freddy had already watched my big black suitcases go around three times, but they didn't know that they belonged to me. I saw them come back around again, and I had Freddy pull them off for me. He placed them on a cart, and I pushed them outside while he went to the parking lot to get the car. Bobbie was still cuddling Vanessa, and I welcomed the time away from her. I'd had enough of her on the plane.

I was very careful pushing the cart because I was already four months pregnant. I didn't want any problems. As soon as we got into the car, Vanessa started to scream. She was not used to such hot and steamy weather. Even though it was December, it felt like June. Freddy turned the A/C on, and I gave Bobbie a bottle for the baby. She closed her eyes and settled down.

The house was about twenty minutes away from the airport, so I didn't have very much time to get it together like I wanted to. I wasn't really ready for the look on Daddy's face when he saw me and my baby girl. Would he be disappointed when he didn't see Jay with us? I knew that I was going to have to answer some questions that I didn't want to. Would Mama know that I was pregnant, even before I told her? She seemed to know those kind of things. I was beginning to feel sick again. At that moment I wished I was back in Detroit.

On the way home we passed the corner where my best friend had lived. I wondered what had happened to her and Ben, a guy that she was having an affair with. Ben was already married when we were playing with baby dolls and jumping rope. I always told her that Ben was a dirty, old man. And what about Sid, did she marry him or did she just stop seeing him? There was so much I wanted to catch up on. She'd stop writing me when I wrote and told her that Jay and I had gotten married.

As Freddy turned into the driveway, I could see everyone gathering around on the front porch waiting for us to come in. The man that lived to the right of our house was outside raking his yard, but he stopped long enough to see who was getting out of the car. The family across the street was sitting on their front porch waiting for me to get out. It felt like I was under a microscope. Everyone seemed to be watching me. My stomach was churning, and my legs felt like Jell-O. I managed to walk from the car to the front porch.

Freddy opened the door for Bobbie and Vanessa, and I walked in behind them. Mama gave me a big hug and said that she was glad that I was back. Then she turned to Bobble and took the baby. The first thing she said was, "This baby looks just like Jay," and everyone agreed. I saw Daddy standing in the living room. I went into the living room to greet him, but the look on Daddy's face reminded me that

I had messed up, and that it was unacceptable. I put my bags down and gave him a big hug anyway. Daddy gave me a pat on the shoulder and told me that Vanessa and I would be sleeping in my old bedroom.

He took the bags to the room and put them down and went back to join the others without saying anything else. Would daddy ever forgive me, I wondered. I hoped that one day I could make it up to him. I put our things away and looked around my old room. I didn't want to start crying, so I went back out and looked around for my baby. I saw her in the living room, and Vanessa was having the time of her little life. She was going from one arm to the next. I just needed my own space for awhile, so I went to sit out on the steps, like I used to do before, when I was home. I couldn't help but think of how things had been before I left home and went to Detroit. I watched the kids playing in the yard. We had shade trees along the street, which formed a green canopy from both sides of the street. Everyone took pride in keeping their yards cut and their houses looking nice; it was a beautiful neighborhood. As I sat there on the steps, I had a flashback to the summer that we first moved into that house.

We had a great time that summer. The neighborhood was clean and safe. The streets were well lit, and we could stay outside after dark as long as we liked. Mama didn't have to worry about where we were because she could see us from our screened porch. There were only about four black families that had moved into the neighborhood. Bobble and I would walk down to the park to see if any of the other black kids were there to talk to. The neighborhood was mostly white. Sometimes we would take our two younger sisters Claire and Kay. We would play games with them if we couldn't find any of the other black kids to talk to. When we did see someone that we knew, we'd put them on the swings while we talked to our friends.

CHAPTER 2

A New Start

I met my best friend Sandy in the park that summer. She and her sister were visiting their dad that summer to see if they liked Miami. Their mom wanted to move to Miami the next year. Her parents had separated three years earlier, and that's when their dad first left South Sueina and moved to Miami. She said that they wanted to go back to Charleston to be with her friends. She and I always hung out at the park, and we would walk to and from Bob's store.

Sandy told me all kind of wild stories about the things she and her friends did when she was back home in Charleston, South Sueina. I thought she knew everything, because she had experienced so much. The only experience I'd had was being able to leave our yard, walk to the park, and go to the store. That summer was the first time for even that to happen. By the end of the summer Sandy said that she would be looking forward to living in Miami when her parents got back together. As if she had a choice. When Sandy went home that summer, I knew she'd be my best friend when she came back.

—◈◈◈—

At least an hour had gone by, and I was still sitting on the steps daydreaming. I got up and went inside. It felt good to see the whole family together again. Even Anne, my older sister, and her family were there. She had twins. Seeing her made me think back to the time when we all lived in the old house together; we were like sardines in a can. Thank God, Daddy found a way to change that.

—◈◈◈—

We moved to another house and left Anne and her family there. My sister Bobbie and I welcomed the change when we moved to 10th Ct. Any change was better than the boring, gloomy and cramped conditions we had to live in, in the old house. Anne got pregnant when she was sixteen. My parents made her get married before the baby was born. She and her husband Al lived there with their little daddy's girl. I had two younger sisters, my mama and daddy, Bobbie and myself. We needed the change from having nine people in a three-bedroom house. Daddy said that Al could pay him the same rent that he had been paying for the room, only they had the whole house. After we moved Anne was not happy with the new arrangements because she had to do her own cooking and take care of her own kids. She also wasn't surrounded by her family anymore.

I felt sorry for Anne, but I also blamed her for making my teenage life miserable with Daddy's Rules: friends could not come over; no friends could call; no parties; no movies; and when the sun went down, we couldn't even go out on the porch. All of the kids in the neighborhood that were male were not allowed to even slow down, look or stop in front of our house. In Daddy's eyes they were all suspects. Mama said that we should try to understand Daddy because he was afraid for us. He didn't want us to make the same mistake that Anne made at our age.

I had a hard time with that. I thought his rules were cruel and inhumane. They didn't think of talking to us about what we shouldn't do. In our house talking about sex was TABOO. They just said, "Don't do it." After we moved to our new neighborhood, things began to change. Maybe not having to see Ann's situation day in and day out made Daddy a little softer. He started to lighten up on the rules. He gave us a little more space to find ourselves, but with a watchful eye.

The summer was over, and it was time to get ready for school. Mama took Claire and Kay to Ann's house so that she could watch them while we shopped for school clothes. Mama already knew what to get the little ones for school from hair ribbons down to their socks and shoes. Bobbie and I were a different case. Our identity was very important to us at that age. Mama had always dressed us in the same clothes when were younger, just different colors. We were determined that we were going to dress to define who we were. Bobbie was about five-feet five, a hundred and ten pounds, light skinned, with shoulder length black hair, and she liked the "Marsha Brady look," from the Brady bunch.

That wasn't quite my style. I was five-feet seven, about one hundred and thirty pounds, dark brown skin. I wore a full afro, with big hoop earrings, and I liked the sweet, brown-sugar look from the Super Fly movies. Mama spent most of the day making us put clothes back on the rack. They were either too expensive or too grown-up looking. But we managed to get through the shopping day without running Mama crazy.

Next, Mama had to get us transferred to another school. She managed to get Claire and Kay into Allapattah Elementary school with no problem. But there was no black Jr. High school in our area yet. Mama had to take us across town to Brownsville Jr. High School. She was worried that it was too far. We would have to catch a city bus to and from school because there was no school bus that would take us across town to school. Mama and Daddy would be at work when we got out of school. It wasn't a big deal to me because catching the city bus meant that I didn't have to go right home after school, and we'd get to see how the people on the other side of town lived.

CHAPTER 3

Exposure

My first day at Brownsville Jr. High School was scary. Most of the students were intercity kids, and they were a little rough around the edges. They grew up in project housing and single parent homes. Most of them had little respect for themselves or the school. Even the girls talked loud in the classrooms and talked back to the teachers. I had never seen students act like them before. In our old neighborhood, the kids that we knew were completely different. They would never do the things that these kids did at Brownsville.

Some of the teachers at Brownsville were passive; they let the students do as they pleased. But Mr. Cook and Mrs. Paste were not one of them. Everyone knew Mr. Cook and Mrs. Paste, and everyone respected them and their classroom. Even the bad kids changed their attitudes when they walked into Cook and Paste's classrooms. Sometimes I was afraid to go to P.E. After we'd change and get into our gym suits, we had to pass the boys' locker room to get to the PE field. The boys would say nasty things to us and grab at us trying to touch our body parts, if their coach wasn't standing right out there. They even told us that they had ways of watching us taking our showers.

But our coach said that they were lying; they had no way of doing such a thing.

After we were in school at least six weeks, Mama realized that she should have placed us in another school. It was a better black school, but it was even further than Brownsville, so we stayed where we were. There was never a dull moment at Brownsville. In just six weeks I learned more about what was going on around me than I did in almost six years under Daddy's Rules in our old neighborhood. But I later learned that Daddy was trying to shelter us from the ugliness of segregation by keeping us in the house. I thought that he was being mean and wanted to keep us locked up all the time. I thought it was awful.

But what was really awful was that segregation was the reason that we had to go all the way to the other side of town to go to school when there was a school right in our neighborhood. I didn't really understand what segregation was all about for a long time. We never really talked about it. Some times I'd hear Daddy say, "That's just how things are in the South, so don't go where white folks don't want you." After I went to Brownsville Jr. High School that year I learned how ugly segregation was. I had never been exposed to it enough to really feel its impact.

One of my teachers was Mr. Cook, who stood about five-feet tall, had smooth, brown skin and wore glasses. He had a voice that would make you sit up and listen. Mr. Cook demanded that we have respect for him and for each other while we were in his classroom. Mr. Cook taught us that we were no better than anyone else, but that we were just as good. Mr. Cook taught English and math, and he kept us in touch with current events each day we went to class. He told us to watch the news more often and to be aware of what was going on around us. Sometimes he would even bring his black and white TV to school so that we could watch the news. Then he would let us discuss how we felt about what we had seen on TV.

I was very upset when I saw black people on the news being beat down and sprayed with water hoses for marching and singing in the street. I felt that it was wrong and that someone needed to go and do something about it. The time was in the sixties, and Martin Luther King led the March on Washington. It was during this time when race riots broke out, and boycotts were being staged, and hundreds of African-Americans were being jailed because of the boycotts. They were being charged with anti-boycott laws. After taking Mr. Cook's class, I was very aware of segregation and its ugliness. It had been segregation that kept black and white students from going to school together, and why racist signs were posted on public facilities. It was segregation that caused some businesses to offer only back-door service to blacks.

When the student in front of me asked about the racist signs, I thought about the time when I was about seven or eight, and we were living in the old neighborhood. We went to the grocery store with our parents, and the store that we went to was one that a classmate of Bobbie's had shopped in with her parents. She told Bobbie that there was a water fountain in that store that had COLORED water and a fountain with WHITE water, but her parents wouldn't let her drink from it.

Bobbie and I decided that when we got inside of the store, we'd get away from Mama so that we could drink from the COLORED fountain. When we got to the back of the store, we saw the water fountains, and while Mama was trying to decide how much meat she could afford, we stood in front of the water fountains. My heart began to race from excitement. I had already imagined seeing the water coming out looking like a rainbow. Or maybe every time I turned the fountain on and off again, the water would be a different color.

When I walked up to drink from the COLORED water fountain, I was very careful not to get any of the COLORED water on my clothes, so I stood back to let only my lips touch the water as it came out. As I turned the fountain on, only clear water came out! I looked back at Bobbie and tried it again. The water was still clear. I was sad and truly disappointed. Then after Bobbie tried it over and over again, she said that the fountain was broken.

We found Mama and walked behind her for a while, and I asked her, "Mama is there another COLORED water fountain in this store?"

"No, Baby, why? Did someone do or say anything to you?"

"No, Mama, I wanted a drink, but I wanted some COLORED water, but the fountain is broken and only clear water comes out."

Mama said, "That's the only kind that's in the water fountain." Then Bobbie explained to Mama that there was a sign that was painted in front of the fountains that read: COLORED, and one that read: WHITE. And Mama was upset. She said that the person that painted those signs was just plain old mean, and that she would explain it to us when we got home.

When we got home, Mama told Daddy that we had to talk, and they told us that the COLORED fountain was for people that were our color, and the WHITE fountain was for people like Mr. Thompson, the milk man. Mama said that we were not allowed to drink from the WHITE fountain because they think that colored people aren't good enough to drink from the same fountain as white people. We didn't really understand, but we didn't want Mama to look so sad anymore, so we acted like we did. Daddy said he knew that we didn't really know what was going on, but when we got older, we'd understand better because we'd go out more.

We hardly ever went with them when they had to shop. In our old neighborhood we never got to see many white people—just the milk man, and the insurance man, and they were both ugly. So Bobbie and I agreed that they should have written UGLY on the WHITE water fountain. But Daddy said that one bad deed did not deserve another. After that day, Daddy never talked about it again.

We also asked Mr. Cook why our text books were always tattered and worn when we received them the first of the school year. He informed us that the school board had a set budget for the white schools and one for black schools. The books that the white schools didn't want anymore or were outdated, the black schools got. This meant that the black students were already one or two years behind the white students, and we wouldn't be able to get into the same colleges because they also knew that we were a year or two behind. Mr. Cook said that we had no time to play around, and that every minute should be put into our school work. I passed Mr. Cook's class in English and math that year.

But what he taught us about civil rights and segregation stuck with me.

I followed the Civil Rights Movement very closely. I even watched the six o'clock news with my parents. I couldn't help but get angry when I saw how blacks were being treated, especially in the South. The following school year, all of Dade County Schools were being integrated. And at the same time, South Florida was being flooded with Cuban immigrants. Most of them made Miami their home. When we went to school that fall, our student body consisted of about 40% white, 30% black, and 30% Cuban.

I didn't know what to expect that year. The first two weeks of school no one talked to me. But I later learned that some of my classmates didn't talk to me because they just didn't want to socialize with me, and the other classmates didn't talk me because they didn't speak English. But they came in all colors and shades; some of them had brown skin color, and some had fair skin like my sister Bobbie. It was hard to tell who was who until I heard them talk, so I didn't talk to anyone. I had to stay focused; I didn't need anything to take my mind off of my school work any way.

I realized that what Mr. Cook had told us about being a couple of years behind the white students, in fact, was true. I was really having a hard time keeping up. I studied extra hard, but my skills were still below my grade level. Two of my teachers informed me and my parents that I had to go to summer school that year in order to pass to the next grade. At first my feelings were crushed; I cried for two days. But the more I thought about it, I realized that they could have just let me repeat that grade, but they gave me a chance to go on the next grade by going to summer school. It was a rough year, but I got through it OK. Thank God.

It was getting later than I had realized, so I turned back towards my house. I had to cross Forty- Six Street, when around the corner came a red convertible with the top down and two men sitting on the trunk. One of them had a microphone announcing, "CASSIUS CLAY, THE NEXT WORLD CHAMP." There were kids following the car chanting, "CASSIUS CLAY is the CHAMP," over and over. Right away I forgot about how late it was, and I joined the crowd and began to chant with them, "CASSIUS is the CHAMP." I had no idea who he was before I heard his name that day. But I was just as excited as everyone else. The crowd was headed in the direction of my house when I remembered that I had to get home.

As I hurried home, a block away from my house, I saw the girl that I'd met in the park the summer before. It was Sandy She was standing on her front porch. She hadn't forgotten my name; she called out, "LOUISE, can you come over?" Happy to see my friend from South Sueina, I ran over to the porch, gave her a hug, and told her how I'd been in the crowd following CASSIUS CLAY'S car, and how we were chanting and everything. That didn't seem to impress her at all.

She told me that they had just gotten in the night before, and that she would be going to school in Miami in the fall, and how she'd have to spend the summer finding the right guy for her boyfriend before school started. Sandy loved to tell long stories, but I had to hurry home because I had never been that late before. I told Sandy to come by if she was going to the park later on that day. I figured maybe Mama would let me go to the park if she came over later.

When I reached the house, I could see Anne's car in the driveway. I could also see her kids running around on the porch. Whenever Anne visited our house with her kids, everything was left in shambles; something was broken or lost and wouldn't be found for days. I always dreaded seeing her car parked in the yard, but that day it was a welcome sight. Her visit took the attention off of me getting home so late. When I went into the house, Mama was in the kitchen. I opened the door to Mama's room and found Anne lying across Mama's bed crying. She hadn't bothered to change into her street clothes. She'd had a fight with her husband Al.

Al was a quiet and gentle man from Sunday until Friday morning. After we all left the old house, Al started drinking heavily. On Friday evenings Al would bring Anne the money for their bills and food. Then he'd get dressed and go out for drinks, and he didn't come back home until Saturday evening. But Anne had been complaining that Al wasn't spending any time with her and the kids. So that Sunday Al took the kids out for a drive and left her home. But on the way back, Al stopped for a drink at the neighborhood bar. He left the kids in the car while he had a few. He'd bought them candy, sodas, and chips to keep them occupied, but once Al started to drink, he had no concept of time.

It was twelve o'clock when Jim, Anne's neighbor, saw the kids asleep in the car. They were sticky and dirty, and mosquitoes were all over them. Jim went into the bar to tell Al about the kids, but Al told Jim to mind his own business. Jim drove to Anne's house and told her what he'd seen and what'd happened. He told her if she wanted him to take her to the bar to just call him.

Jim always liked Anne, even when we all lived in that house together. Sometimes if we were all out on the porch with Anne, Jim would drive by and see Anne. He'd stop and ask if she wanted anything from the store. (Al, Mama and Daddy would still be at work.) Sometimes she'd say she wanted something, and we'd all put in an order for sodas and chips or cookies. We all liked Mr. Jim. He was a tall, brown-skinned man and very nice looking. He was about 27 or 28 yrs old. Anne was about 18. She'd always say that Jim was too old for her.

Anyway, Al came back with the kids an hour later. Anne said that the kids had mosquito bites all over their bodies, and they had peed until they were soaked. And Al just put them in the bed and went to sleep himself. Anne said that Al had to go, or she was leaving. I tried to convince Anne to put Al out. I couldn't bare the thought of them moving in with us, but Mama came in and told me to get out, she had to talk to Anne. I didn't say a word. I was ready to leave anyway; I wanted to go to the park with Sandy when she came by.

By the time I got changed and walked outside, I saw Sandy walking toward our house. She was dressed comfortably too. Sandy was about five-feet eight, and our weight was about the same. Her skin color was black and smooth; her afro was cute, but not as full as mine. She had a walk that could turn the guys' heads, but to me it looked nasty. When Sandy got in front of my house, we walked to the park together. I couldn't wait to hear more of her wild stories about how she was able to control the guys and make them do what she wanted them to. But I didn't know if I liked the sound of that. I wanted a date, not a puppet. So I asked, "Sandy, how can you control what a guy wants to do?"

"With sex! Girl, never tell them that you're a virgin!"

What's that? I thought to myself, it's something she made up. That's right I'd been in the house so long, under Daddy's Rules so long, I didn't even know what a virgin was!

"Girl, how long has your mama been keeping you in that house?" She began to laugh uncontrollably; she even fell off her swing. What could be so funny, I thought? She told me what a virgin was. Even if I was a virgin, what was so wrong with that? And why would I have to use sex to have control over a guy?

"Well, if you are going to be hanging out with me," she said, "you've got a lot to learn."

"Learn about what?" I asked.

"Ok. What did you and your last boyfriend do when you went out?"

"What boyfriend?" I answered. "I won't be able to date until I'm sixteen, so you have to teach me what I need to know," I pleaded.

"Well, we are going to have to get you a boyfriend before your birthday, because you need some experience. You can take him home and let your mama check him out later."

I often wondered how and when did Sandy have time to get so much experience, and where was her mother when it was all happening. I couldn't imagine her mother just letting her do all of those things that she said she'd been doing unless Florida parents and South Sueina parents raise their kids differently. The bottom line was that Sandy lied a lot, but I still liked listening to her stories. We spent most of our summer at the park telling stories and flirting with the boys. Sometimes I would give out the right phone number and another name, or the right name and the wrong phone number. I knew that I couldn't have boys calling the house asking to speak to Louise. That was the perfect way to get myself put back on lock-down, and I never wanted to see those days ever again. I was just having fun, not going crazy.

After all I was not yet sixteen, and one of Daddy's Rules was, as he would put it, "If you get your lessons, maybe you can have a couple of phone calls when you're sixteen." No dates, no going to the movies, and no talking to boys. In a few months I would be sixteen, and I'd planned to sort of change some of Daddy's Rules. But for the summer I just pretended that there were no Daddy's Rules and that I was in control just like Sandy, that is until I went home.

In two weeks we would be going back to school for the fall, and I still didn't have a special someone to be with yet. Sandy had said that we had to have a boyfriend when we started school for the fall. It was just like having to have a new notebook for class. I told Sandy that I wasn't that serious about having that special person when I went back to school because I wanted to stay on top of my studies. I was sure that I would get side-tracked trying to deal with a boyfriend for the first time, and trying to keep it from Daddy. I didn't want to have to go back to summer school again.

The next few days I didn't see Sandy at the park, and she was never home when I called her on the phone. I knew that she was avoiding me, so I started spending more time at the park with my two younger sisters. I later learned that Sandy had spent the rest of her summer dating one of the guys that she had met at the park. I ran into them one day when I had Claire and Kay at the park. I could see Sandy and her boyfriend over at the picnic tables playing cards and drinking beer. I couldn't believe my eyes. It must be someone that looks like Sandy, I thought. While Claire and Kay were on the swings, I went over to the table to make sure it was her, and sure enough it was. When she looked up and saw that it was me, she offered me a beer. I said, "No thanks."

I never would have thought that I'd see Sandy out in the park drinking alcohol with guys she'd just met weeks before. She was moving a little too fast for me. I didn't try to contact Sandy after that. She'd try to call me, but I stayed clear of her the rest of the summer. Sandy had disappointed me, and I knew she realized it. I hoped she'd change her habits.

School started that fall, and I was going to be a sophomore. I was really proud of myself. My sister Bobbie was going to be a junior.

Miami Jackson Sr. High School had opened its doors to Blacks and Hispanics, and we were going to be a part of its integrated student body. They also offered as an elective, Spanish classes, for those who qualified. Bobbie took Spanish as one of her electives. She loved the language; she said that she loved the way the Latinos sounded when they talked. Bobbie was at the top of her Spanish class that year; she made all A's.

She also made friends with some of the Latino kids. Sometimes when I'd pass her in the hall, she'd be in the mist of her new-found, Latino friends speaking their language. She'd never even notice me passing her. Sometimes I'd feel left out or jealous, but most of the time I'd be flirting with the guys as I went to my next class, even though I'd promised myself that I was going to stay on top of my classes. It was hard to think about math with all of the male attention walking around, but I managed.

My birthday had come and gone. I was already sixteen and was allowed to take phone calls. I'd also made new friends other than Sandy, who thought she had all of the answers when it came to the guys. I still hung out with her sometimes, even though we didn't see eye to eye on a lot of things. I noticed that Bobbie and I had stopped hanging out together; we didn't do things together the way we used to. We were allowed to do things that we couldn't do before, as far as Daddy's Rules were concerned, but we never did any of them together. We had started to run in different circles, and we had different values. We had even stopped talking when we were at home. The whole school year went by like that. I met a couple of nice guys and found some new friends. And Bobbie had learned the Latinos' culture and was becoming one.

When school ended that year I had to go to summer school again. I needed to take an extra math class if I wanted to be on the same level of math as the other juniors the next school year. Bobbie went to summer school also that summer. She took conversational Spanish, even though she was already speaking Spanish fluently. The summer just flew by. When we were not in summer school, we were hanging out with our separate circle of friends. Even though I had my little circle of friends, I missed my sister. I missed sharing secrets, playing around in our room before we went to bed, and talking about how inhumane Daddy's Rules were. We hardly talked about anything, and when we did, we were disagreeing about something. We had always been so close, and when we started to grow apart like that, it made me sad.

Mama and Daddy were really concerned about our behavior also. I tried to tell them what was happening, but they said that I was just jealous because Bobbie had Spanish friends and could speak Spanish with them, and I didn't. I didn't even try to defend myself because I knew that it was a fight that I'd never win. When school opened the next fall, one week before registration Bobbie transferred to another school. It broke my heart, but I didn't let anyone know how much she'd hurt me. But then as far as I was concerned, we weren't sisters anymore. She'd begun to act like them.

We had a fight because I told her that she couldn't pass for white, so she was trying to pull it off as a Latino. Because in her eyes, anything was better than being black. I was punished for what I'd said, but that's how I felt. I was so mad at my Daddy that I could just spit. I thought to myself he'd never understand me, and that Daddy didn't like me because I was the dark one. But then that didn't make much sense, because Mama was as black as I was, and Daddy LOVED Mama. Then I thought he just didn't like me. Weeks went by, and we were strangers in our own home.

By Thanksgiving Bobbie was dating Latino guys. When they came to our house to take her out, Mama and Daddy pulled out the red carpet, and they were greeted with smiles. They didn't even ask the guys where they were going, and they didn't even mention what time she had to be back. When my friends came to pick me up, they got a different treatment. Daddy jacked the guy up and told him where he better not take me, and Mama stamped the "I should be home by," on my forehead. Well, maybe I exaggerated a bit, but they may as well have done that too with the way they treated us. They said that I made bad choices, and that the guys that I brought home were from the projects, and that was not a good thing.

When I brought Walter home, I told him how my parents were. I told him what to say and how to say it, and whatever he did, not to say that he was from the projects. I liked Walter; I wanted to go out with him again, so he had to pass the test. (That was Sandy's idea; sometimes she was good for something.) Daddy had his reservations about Walter, but he did pass the test. We dated for a while, even though Daddy said there was something about him that he didn't like.

Anyway that year our high school had a winning football team. We had a few black players on our team, and the Jackson Generals were kicking butt. For our Thanksgiving games we were going to play the Miami Edison Caviliers, the same school that Bobbie had transferred to. Bobbie and I were at each other's throat everyday boasting about whose team was going to win. Everyone kept boosting us up because they were glad that we were at least talking. We had not talked to each other that much the whole school year. The school that Bobbie went to had a pretty good team too. The Latino boys were holding their own as well. Everyone said that it would be a good game because they were two good teams. Bobbie and I made a pact. Whoever's team won would have to wash the dishes for a month and come in the house after school by walking all the way around the house and coming in through the kitchen.

CHAPTER 4

The Thanksgiving Game

The night of the game, my friend Walter and Bobbie's friend Rico arrived at our house about the same time. They knocked on the door. They both smiled and shook Daddy's hand, but they both hated each other, even though they acted as if everything was OK while they were in front of Daddy. When Bobbie and I came out, we got our coats and were on our way out the door when Daddy stopped all of us to remind us of his rules and to make sure that our dates understood what time to have us home. Daddy looked at Walter the whole time that he was talking, as if the rules were only for Walter's benefit, while Rico smiled. I had to bite my lip to keep from saying anything because I really wanted to go to the game that night. Daddy excused himself and went into his room. We all said goodnight while Mama let us out and locked the door behind us. We got into our cars and went to the game.

The score in the first quarter was (7-6) Generals favor. The second quarter, the score was (21- 20) still our favor, but one of the Generals got hurt really bad. I just knew that I was going to be washing dishes for a month then because Sims, the injured player, was one of our key players for the Generals. The coach replaced him with # 99, Sidney

Bear. All the kids at school called Sid, "99." (His jersey # was 99, and that's the name he answered to around school.) "99" was fast, and once he got the ball, he was unstoppable. He gave the Generals a sweet victory that night. I was so happy I couldn't stop screaming. We had won the game, and Bobbie had to wash dishes for a month.

As Walter and I walked to his car, he asked me if I'd like to go to a victory party at his house that night. Everyone seemed to know about the party and where it was. We all drove over to the 62nd Street Projects. I could hear the music even before I got to his apartment. When I got inside, I met Walter's family. We all had to try to talk over the music, but no one seemed to mind. I'd never been to a party like that before. I had been sixteen for only a month, so I had not been to a party before, thanks to Daddy's Rules. I was having a blast until I saw Rico's friend, China. He came over and asked me for a dance. Just as I was turning him down, Walter walked up with my soda. He recognized China as being one of Rico's friends, and he told him to leave. I was glad that he left without causing any trouble. The rest of the night was great. It was the best time I'd ever had!

The next week I imagined Bobbie washing dishes and having to enter the house from the back door. But by the next week, Rico's friend had told him what had happened at the party, and Rico told Bobbie. That night Bobbie came into the room smiling and told me that if I didn't start washing dishes for her the next night that she would tell Daddy what Rico had told her about where Walter lived, and that Rico's friend had seen me at a party in the projects with Walter after the Thanksgiving game. And that his friend would confirm it if he had to.

My first reaction was to choke the breath out of her. But I managed to control my anger. I thought about it for a while and chose not to let her have control over me through her little blackmail scam. I went to the closet to find something to wear to school the next day. I didn't even respond to what Bobbie was saying to me. She walked over to the closet where I was standing and said, "Don't even try to act like you didn't know where Walter lived."

"I didn't. I found out when I met his family at the victory party after the Thanksgiving game."

"Louise, I know you don't expect me to believe that."

"I don't care what you believe. It's the truth, and that's why I'm not seeing Walter anymore." I knew that once Bobbie told Daddy what Rico had told her, Walter would not be welcome in our house anymore. I had to break it off with Walter the next day after school. I only wished I had a better reason than that, but at the time I couldn't think of the smallest reason why I had to break Walter's heart. I figured it was better if he heard it from me than from Daddy.

The next day whenever I saw Walter in the hall as we changed classes, I'd just wave at him and go on to class. If we had a class together, I didn't have much to say. I was trying to think of how I was going to tell him. When I met Walter after school, he looked upset. He wanted me to give him my books so that he could carry them home for me, but I refused. He wanted to know what was wrong—had he done anything to make me mad at him. I told Walter that he had not done anything wrong, but as we got to the corner where I lived, I asked him not to walk me to my door. Then I told that I had to break it off with him. I didn't bother telling him about Rico and about Bobbie and the blackmailing, because it would have been a big mess. Walter still would not have been welcome at our house, and I would have been grounded for life.

Walter kept asking me what he'd done. He even accused one of the guys in our class of trying to hit on me, and he thought that was why I wanted to get him out of the way. Walter was talking about Rick, who was a guy in my English class. He liked to tease me about getting married just to get on Walter's nerves. Sometimes he'd ask me to a party or a dance, and I'd laugh and tell him to stop acting crazy. Walter hated him. Anyway the more I tried to assure him that that wasn't it, the more upset he seemed to get. At that point I turned and began to walk home. Walter wanted to follow me, but I told him that I didn't want him at my house and to please go home.

The next day at school he followed me around trying to talk to me. I tried not to be mean to Walter, but it was the only way I could get him to leave me alone. The next day he picked a fight with the guy that he said was trying to hit on me and got a three-day suspension. Although I was the one who broke it off with Walter, I missed him walking me home after school, talking to him on the phone, and going out with him on the weekends. I didn't have Walter anymore, but I sure had fun watching Bobbie wash dishes for a whole month. She never said anything about Walter living in the projects and about how China saw me at the victory party. I guess she knew that she would look like a little snitch since Walter wasn't coming around anyway.

The holidays rolled around—the best time to be with the one you love. Every time a Christmas song came on like, "Gee Wiz It's Christmas," I thought about Walter. The holidays were hard for me that year. I think I must have cried every night from Christmas Eve 'til New Year's night. After the holidays, and even that spring, I spent a lot of time in the park enjoying the weather and just thinking. The weather was beautiful, our usual tropical Florida weather. One evening in March, after spending some time at the park enjoying my own company, I took a slow walk back home. When I got to the front of the house, I could see Daddy standing in front of the TV. I hurried inside to see what he was watching. When Daddy stood up in front of the TV, it was a sign that he was not happy about what he was watching.

When I got inside, he was watching the news, and they were doing a report about two, new black leaders speaking out for the black community: Malcolm X and the Black Panthers. They were demanding Civil Rights, but NOT a non- violent approach. Daddy was upset because he didn't approve of anything that the new leaders had to say. He also had a frown on his face that showed it. "Trouble makers, that's what they are, trouble makers." Then Mama came in to see why Daddy was getting so upset.

After listening to the news for awhile, Mama wanted to know where the leaders came from. "Where do they live, Robert? I hope they don't start no trouble down here." Mama stood there with a worried look on her face.

"No, Baby. They up north with that sh——. All them niggers up there are crazy as hell." Daddy's face had turned red, and he looked as though someone had personally offended him.

Daddy never liked trouble. He never taught us to hate anyone because of their race or color. He said that we should treat everyone as individuals. Daddy said that the white racists and the black militants were both wrong. He said that President Kennedy and Dr. King were the only leaders that were smart enough for us to follow.

I turned and looked at both of them in total amazement. I couldn't believe the things that they were saying. I was so mad with them. I was steaming; I really wanted to let them have it. But I knew it was no use talking to Daddy about how I felt about the situation. His mind was already made up: they were trouble makers! If I had voiced any other opinion, I would have been grounded for life. After that day, I focused all of my attention on our new leaders and the Civil Rights Movement. The circle of friends that I hung around with at that time had no interest in the movement. Their only interest was dating, clothes, parties and sometimes sex. I knew that it was time for me to move on. I had outgrown my friends. I walked in the park by myself a lot; I did most of my thinking there. I wanted to know how the Black Panthers had gotten started.

CHAPTER 5

When I Met Jay

One night my cousin came by the house with her date. His friend had come along just for the ride. At least that's what they told me, but I knew that it was a setup from the start. Then Neeka, my cousin, asked me if I'd like to go to a Super Fly movie. Neeka knew that I'd never turn down a chance to see Super Fly. Daddy had come into the living room as Neeka was introducing everyone. Neeka's friend's name was Eddie Jackson. Everyone in the family knew Eddie; Neeka talked about Eddie to anyone who'd listen. But when she introduced Jay Cob, my ears perked up, and so did Daddy's.

We learned that Jay was a Viet-Nam vet, a student of Florida A & M University, and he was home on spring break. He was also born here in Miami. His family still lived in Opa-Locka. A smile moved across Daddy's face as he looked at me. He had already figured that they'd brought Jay there for me to double date with them, When I asked Daddy if it was OK for me to go to the movies with them, he said it was OK, without a fuss. I could tell that Daddy was impressed with Jay. I went into the room to change. When I came out, they were ready to go. We all said goodnight to Daddy and headed for the door.

Jay caught up with me and whispered in my ear, "Don't look so serious. I don't bite." I smiled and walked ahead of him. I had a feeling that we had made a connection somehow, even though Neeka had set the whole thing up. We all went to the movies and had a great time. After the movies, we drove back to my house and parked the car right out front. Neeka's friend Eddie got his portable radio out of the back of his car, and we all walked down the street to the park. It was still early, and the night air was cool and refreshing. The street lamps gave off just enough light, shining down on the park benches, just in case someone wanted to have a private moment to talk or to cuddle. Jay and I found a bench suited just for us, and we spent the rest of the time we had left just talking about things we liked and disliked.

Jay asked me what I was most interested in, and I told him about my search for more information about Malcolm X, The Black Panthers, and the Civil Rights Movement. And I found that Jay was very knowledgeable about all three subjects. Jay knew the answer to all of my questions, and he cleared up all of my uncertainties. He explained to me how Malcolm X broke away from the Nation of Islam and formed the OAAU and how he'd set out to bring charges against humanity before the United Nations, and against the United States. Then Jay leaned back and laid his arm on the back of the bench. He looked at me and asked if he was talking too much. I said, "No." I wanted to know more about the Black Panthers. Because I had only heard about their boldness and arrogance, I wanted to know what they were really like. I couldn't let Jay change the channel on me yet. I wanted to know more, and he told me more.

Jay said that two young brothers from the West coast started the Panther Movement: Bobby Seals and Huey Newton. They were in college, and they were influenced by Malcolm X's stance on self-defense, and they called themselves the children of Malcolm because of his philosophy. Jay said that the Panthers were misrepresented, and that the public was misinformed by the media. Jay also said not to forget about Dr. Martin Luther King Jr. He said that Dr. King was telling everyone to wake up. It's a new day. Stop the backwards thinking and move on.

We must have talked for about an hour when Neeka and Eddie walked up smiling. They seemed to be pleased to see Jay and me getting along so well. Jay stood up and took my hand when I got up. We started walking toward my house. Neeka and Eddie walked ahead of us. We told each other how much we enjoyed the night and agreed to see each other again. Jay and I went out a few times before he had to go back to college.

After getting to know each other well, Jay brought his sister Joy over to meet me. Joy was very pleasant, and we liked each other. She was about 15, but she was about 25 mentally and physically. Jay would be going back to school in two weeks. He'd call me or I'd call him because we didn't have much time with each other. The days were passing fast. We often talked about how much we'd miss each other once Jay went back to school. Joy and I planned to give him a going away party since he would be leaving soon. So we had to get started planning everything.

Saturday night came before we realized it, and we had to get everything together without Jay knowing about it. We wanted it to be a surprise. It was hard, but we managed to pull everything off. On the night of the party, I noticed that Joy and her older sister Susan were fighting about everything. It made me realize how my sister Bobbie and I must have looked when other people saw us fighting. Sure we had our issues, but I loved my sister. After that night, I didn't want to fight with her anymore.

Finally, it was time for Jay to go back to school. He came over the night before he had to leave. We talked for awhile and said our last good byes. We promised to write each other often. Having a distant lover was something new to me, and since dating was just as new, I wondered if we were supposed to see other people or what. Not that I wanted to see anyone, but I didn't want Jay to date anyone else either. I just hoped he wouldn't. The first two weeks, I wrote Jay a letter every other day. Three weeks passed, and I had not heard from Jay. He didn't write or even call. I had so many sleepless nights wondering what had happened. I had let this person into my space and into my heart, and he'd forgotten about me. At least that's what my mind was telling me, but my heart was saying something different. I prayed that he'd call to just let me know what was going on. I didn't know what to do. So I called my friend Sandy. She always had an answer for couples that were having problems. She always knew what to do.

"Hey Girl, it's Louise. I haven't heard from Jay since he left. He hasn't written What do you think, Sandy?"

"You should have made sure that you slept with him before he left, for one thing, and you wouldn't be having this problem." She boasted.

"I don't even know why I called you, Sandy. Your solution to every problem is sex."

The next week Jay's sister called me. I was really glad to hear from her, but at the same time I didn't want her to know that I was going out of my mind not knowing what was going on with Jay. Not hearing from him for weeks, I'd imagined all sorts of things. Had he gotten sick or just forgotten about our relationship? The more she talked, the more upset I got. But I managed to stay cool. She may have detected a little attitude in my voice, but I didn't care. Jay had hurt me, and I guess I just wanted to take it out on somebody. So why not, Joy?

She said that Jay had quit school and had gone to Detroit. Their uncle had gotten sick and needed Jay to come up there and help run their night club. She also said that Jay had only called them the night before. Joy said that Jay had missed me and wanted to talk to me. Joy said she knew that was the only reason he was calling them, because he wanted her to get that message to me.

"So why didn't your uncle call your mom or your dad, why Jay?" "That's the way it is in our family. Everyone depends on Jay." "But what about your dad?" I asked.

"What about him? He doesn't care. My uncles are my mother's family."

"Did Jay say when he was coming back to Miami?" I asked.

"I'm glad you asked that question. Jay will be back in two weeks, and he wants to know if you'll call him. I have the number for you."

"Why doesn't he call me?" I asked.

"You'll have to ask him, Louise. I don't know."

Joy gave me the number. I said, "Thanks," and hung up the phone. I was so happy I started to dance around the room. I waited a few days before I called him. I went over and over in my head just what I was going to say to him. I kept thinking to myself when I do call Jay, I won't be easy on him. And this time around, he won't get a chance to hurt me, ever again. I waited until that weekend when everyone in the house was busy doing housework. I found the number in my purse and called collect. The operator picked up. I told her that I was calling person to person to a Mr. Jay Cob. She made our connection and said, "Go ahead, please."

"Hello, Louise, is that you?" His voice sounded like he was glad to hear from me." I was excited to hear his voice too. Tears were falling down my face as I tried so hard to sound tough, and as if I didn't care. I didn't want Jay to know I'd missed him and how he'd hurt me.

"Yeah it's me. Joy said you wanted me to call. So what's up?" "You sound like you are mad. What's wrong, Babe?"

"What's W-R-O-N-G!!? Jay, you didn't write or even call for almost a month, and you want to know what's wrong?" I cried. I was in tears. I couldn't talk, so I stop trying to. Then there was silence on the phone for almost five minutes before Jay said anything.

"I know, I know, Babe. When I left school to come here, I wanted to call you, but then I didn't know how serious you were about me.

So I didn't call you. I thought that since I wasn't there, you may have wanted to see other people. I let my pride get in the way. But after a while I couldn't even concentrate on what I was doing here. And I've realized that I can't do without you. Please give me another chance?" I didn't want Jay to think that it was going to be that easy for me to forgive him. But I had, I had forgiven Jay the moment I heard his voice.

"Well, how is your uncle?" I wouldn't say if I would give him another chance or not. I left it for him to wonder about.

"You didn't hang up, and I see that you are still talking to me, so does that mean that I'm forgiven? Will you give me another chance?"

"Don't push it, Jay." We laughed and said how much we'd missed each other.

We had one phone, and it was in the living room. My family had no shame when it came to listening to others' conversations. Since everyone found a reason to wander into that area, I couldn't say too much more. The whole house seemed to have gotten quiet. Everyone with ears was listening to my phone conversation. So I let Jay do most of the talking. He told me when he was returning to Miami and when he would be over to visit me. Then he said, "Love you."

I smiled and said, "Love you too." We didn't want to, but we hung up. I thought about Jay all that week. I couldn't eat. I couldn't sleep or concentrate on anything! I'd never felt that way about Walter. It was then I realized how much I loved Jay.

CHAPTER 6

One Week Later

The next week Jay called me. He was back in Miami and wanted to come over to visit me, but it was already nine o'clock at night and a school night. Daddy had already let me take the call, and one of his rules was, no calls after nine. I didn't want to push it. I pleaded with Jay not to come over because he'd start a riot if he did. Jay laughed and said that he'd come over around seven o'clock the next night, which would be a Friday night. That would be even better.

The next day in school all I could think about was Jay. I was on cloud nine and nothing could bring me down. While I was in my English class, I found myself day dreaming, and half way through the class, my teacher put me out for not paying attention. And I didn't even care. Any other day being put out of class would have been the worst thing that could have ever happened to me. But that day it just gave me more time to think about Jay. So I got my books together, smiled and walked out of class. I went downstairs, and I walked out of the building.

Across the street there was a soda and coffee shop, a sandwich shop, and a five and dime. I could see that they were beginning to get busy. I headed for the soda shop, so I could sit there and think of what it was going to be like when I saw Jay that night. As I crossed the street, I heard a horn blowing non-stop. When I turned around, it was a green Eldorodo with gangster white walls, an antenna on the back, and a handsome face hanging out the driver's window waving and calling my name. I hurried across the street and looked again, It was Jay's smiling face. I could have just dropped, I was so surprised. As I reached the curb on the other side, I could see Jay parking the car down the street. I began to walk to where he had parked the car. As I got closer, Jay had already gotten out of the car, and we were both smiling from ear to ear. When we met, Jay bent over and gave me a big hug and turned me around and around so hard that my shoe came off.

"What are you doing here at school, Jay?"

"I was going to wait there in front of the school until you got out for lunch," he explained.

"But we said that we were going to see each other tonight at seven."

"Oh yeah! I'm still coming at seven. But I couldn't wait that long to see you. You know we won't have any private time together when I come to your house tonight. They'll be watching and listening to everything we do and say. And I really want some time with you alone." Jay was right. We did need some time together because when he visited me that night, we were going to be "on stage." Jay took my hand and walked me back to the car. As we walked back, I could hear the lunch bell rang, and it seemed like students poured out of the school and across the street. Some of my classmates waved at me, and I waved back. They noticed that Jay was not some school-age boy, and he wasn't from around here. And I was proud that he was with me.

We got into his car, and we talked and listened to music through my lunch period. Jay had several eight-track tapes on the front seat. He put in one of them. It was by the Originals. "Baby I'm for Real" came on first. He turned the music up and started to sing to me, and when I started to blush, he leaned over and kissed me. My head was really in the clouds then. The school bell rang again; it was time to go back to class. Jay drove around the corner and then back in front of the school and let me out.

I went to my next class, and on the way I saw my best friend Sandy and her first words were, "I saw you get into a strange car today; who was he?"

Sandy was my best friend, but she had no shame when it came to other people's business. She had watched me cross the street that morning when my English teacher had put me out of class. She could see me from the upstairs, hall window in front of the school. From that window you could see everything that went on around the school and the whole block outside. Sandy had watched me leave the building, cross the street, and walk to Jay's car. She even watched Jay and me hug each other. But she didn't know who Jay was, from where she was standing. She had no idea that he was back in Miami, and she also didn't recognize the car he was driving. She thought that I had found a new friend, and that I had skipped class to meet him.

I told Sandy that I didn't have time to explain at the moment, but that I'd tell her everything after school that day.

It was three o'clock, and Sandy was standing at the door of my classroom. It was my last class, and I was thinking about Jay again. When Mrs. Grant saw Sandy standing at the door, she told me to get out because she knew that Sandy was waiting for me, and that I was disturbing her class. Well, she didn't have to tell me twice, I was up and out of there.

As Sandy and I started to walk home, I told her that I got put out of class that morning and why. I also told her who was in the car that she didn't recognize. I hadn't told her earlier that Jay was in town because I had not seen her yet. I told her that Jay and I had talked on the phone the night before and agreed to see each other that night at seven, but Jay said that he couldn't wait that long. Then she said, "So what did you two talk about? Are you going to do it?"

"Do what Sandy?" Knowing what she was trying to say, I rolled my eyes. "Are you going to have sex tonight? What else?"

"Is that all you think about? We have other things to discuss."

"Well, don't say I didn't warn you. If you don't do it, he'll leave you."

"Then if sex is all he's about, he can leave." I walked faster, leaving Sandy a few steps behind. The rest of our walk home was quiet; there was silence for two blocks. I was glad that Sandy wasn't talking because she had pissed me off with all the talk about sleeping with Jay. Why did she think that was so important? It was times like this when I wished Bobbie and I were closer and talking to each other, so we could figure out what I would do if sex came up while I was dating Jay. I needed to know because even the word "sex" was not allowed in our home. If Daddy ever heard any of us mention "sex" we'd be grounded for life.

When we got to the next block, it was where Sandy turned off to go home, and she said to me, "Louise, think about what I said." I didn't even bother to answer. I hurried home, changed my clothes, and began my house duties. I didn't want Mama to find any reason to say that I couldn't have company come over that night.

It was six-thirty, and I'd just come out of the bathroom. I noticed my sister Bobbie getting dressed too. She smiled and turned around for me to zip her dress. Then she said that Rico was taking her to a party. She asked me what I was going to do. I said I had not decided yet. It really didn't matter what we did that night, I had already spent personal time with Jay earlier that day, and maybe it would be a good idea to stay around the house and let the family watch us all night. It'd give them a chance to know him better. They were already camped out in the living room waiting for him to come in. Everyone had a ring-side seat. By the time I got dressed, Bobbie had already left. I heard someone bumping around in the living room. It was my little sisters looking out the window watching Jay walk to the house from his car.

Jay was a guy any girl could be proud of. He was six-feet tall, about 180 lbs., pecan tan, with an afro that was cut just right for his face, and wide shoulders that made the rest of his body look perfect. I heard Mama say that Jay was a handsome young man. Then Claire came to my room door and said, "Louise someone's here to see you."

"OK, I'm coming," I answered. I went to the door and let Jay into the house. He smiled, and I smiled back. I took Jay's hand and lead him to the far corner of the living room. As we passed through, I introduced him to everyone again.

By the time we were seated, Daddy came in from the kitchen and said, "Hey, Son, how you doing?"

"Just fine, Sir." Jay stood up while he was talking to Daddy. Daddy said the first time he met Jay, he liked him because he was raised right.

"How long are you going to be here?" Daddy asked. "I'm really not sure, Sir."

"Well, anyway, it's good to see you again." Daddy went into his room and closed the door. Mama came back into the living room and changed the channel. They always watched "The Fugitive." It was the episode when they caught the one-armed man. Although my eyes were on the TV, I still got a glimpse of everyone watching us. When the commercial came on, Jay and I went out on the porch to talk.

We had an old couch on our front porch that used to be in the living room of our old house. It sat against the wall facing the street. The porch was screened, so we had a good view of almost everything on our street. There was a glass door that closed the porch off from the living room, and Mama had made some curtains to put up to the door, so that no one could see inside the house from the porch. This meant no one could see out on the porch from inside the house. So Jay and I cuddled and kissed on the porch.

"So Jay, when are you going back to Detroit?"

"As soon as I know that everything is alright between us. I want you to tell me that you have forgiven me. And I can go when I know that we love each other." It had pleased me to know that Jay had come all the way to Miami because he was that concerned about our relationship.

"Jay, as long as we communicate while you're gone, no problem."

"You don't have to worry. I'll never be that stupid again." Jay took both of my hands and folded them into his. He looked so serious.

"What's wrong, Jay?" I asked.

"Babe, I'll be leaving in a few days. I just want to know that I'm your only man."

"Jay, if you are worried about me cheating on you, then don't be, because I won't." He pulled me into his arms and kissed me, and I kissed him back. I didn't care who was looking. I got a warm sensation all over my body every time Jay touched me. I didn't know what was going on, so I pushed him off of me. I told Jay that things were getting a little too hot and that I'd better go in. He agreed.

"Hey! Let's go to the drive-in movie tomorrow," he suggested. Jay wanted to get onto another subject. We both knew what could have happened at another place and time, but we didn't want to get into it.

"Sure, what's playing?" I said, as I tried to get my body to shake that sensation that it still had.

"'Three the Hard Way,' is playing." "I hear that it's a good flick."

"OK, I'll pick you up at six."

"Wait. I'll have to ask my parents first, then I'll call you tomorrow." Jay gave me a peck on the cheek, got into his car and drove off.

I opened the door and sat out on the steps. I needed to process what had happened earlier when Jay kissed me the way he did. It made me feel so good inside. Every time I had a flashback, I felt it all over again, and I liked it. We had an old beat-up radio sitting on the porch. I opened the screen door on the porch. (We kept the radio in the window.) I stuck my hand inside the screen door, and I turned it on. Barbara Mason had just cut a new record called, "Yes, I'm Ready." It was perfect for the mood I was in. I'd even thought about what Sandy had said earlier that day about sleeping with Jay. I had no idea of what to do, but I was ready to learn.

As I sat there on the steps I observed how the street lamps lined up with the houses. And the trees overlapped each other, covering the streets as far as I could see; it seemed to be never-ending. It looked just beautiful. My back was turned to the screen door. I knew Mama was coming to the door to see how I was doing and why I was still sitting there. I could hear her slippers flopping across the tile floor. Mama was concerned that Jay had gone, and I was still out side. Mama knew that's where I did a lot of my thinking. Sometimes I think Mama knew more about us than we realized.

"Girl, is everything alright?" Mama asked. "Yes, Ma. Everything's alright."

"Why are you sitting out here all by yourself?"

"I'm waiting for Sandy; she said that she'd drop by later." I lied. I had to tell Mama something, so she'd stop asking questions. I could never tell her about the flashbacks I was having about Jay and me.

"Louise, I wish you wouldn't hang around with that Sandy girl. She's not the kind of girl you should be with. Her own mama told me a thing or two about her." I knew what Mama was saying. I'd already seen Sandy in action.

I heard more foot steps coming toward us; it was Daddy. "Everything alright out there, girls?" Daddy was concerned too.

"Yeah, everything's OK." "Where is that boy?"

"Jay left early tonight. Daddy, he wants to take me to the movies tomorrow.

Can I go?"

"OK. You can go, but be back here by twelve."

Did Daddy say "twelve o'clock?" He surprised me. He must really like Jay. He gave us an extra hour. I thought… maybe I'm making progress with DADDY'S RULES. I got up from the steps and joined them in the living room; we watched the rest of the news and went to bed.

The next day was Saturday, and we were all doing our weekly chores. Bobbie and I were cleaning our room and listening to the radio. It came on again, Barbara Mason singing "Yes, I'm Ready." I loved that song. I started singing to myself and pretending that I was talking to Jay.

"What are you so happy about?" Bobbie asked. I didn't answer her. I kept singing. "I know you are glad that Jay is home, huh? You know, Louise, he's not going to stay. He's going back to Detroit."

"Not that it's any of your business, but I know that."

"What kind of a relationship is that? He's in Detroit, and you are here?"

"Look, it's not your problem, so don't worry about it. I'm not."
"I'm not worried. I'm just telling you, it's not going to work."

I shook my dust rag at Bobbie and shouted over the music, "Stay out of my business."

"OK, you don't have to be so nasty."

I just went into another room because it was not a good time to get into a fight with her. I felt bad for shouting. Maybe she just wanted to talk like sisters. Sometimes I didn't know how to take her. Bobbie was confused about her identity and in denial of who she was, but she was my sister, and I still loved her.

CHAPTER 7

A Date to Remember

It was Saturday night, a really big night for Jay and me. It would be the first time we could "really" be together since he had returned from Detroit. No one to look over our shoulders, I was excited. When I started to get dressed I wanted to look mature, but not so grown-up that Mama would embarrass me. I finally put together something that Jay might like, and it made me feel mature at the same time. I wanted to smell just as nice. Sandy had given me some perfume that smelled just heavenly, but I'd have to wait until I was out of the house to put it on. Meanwhile Mama and the rest of the family were watching the clock and looking out of the window waiting for Jay to drive up. I often wondered why everyone had to be in on my business.

Then I heard Daddy saying, "Is that girl dressed yet?" I opened the door and yelled, "I'm almost dressed."

Then Mama opened the door and asked, "You dressed yet? That boy is here." Why did they always have to say, "that boy?" Why couldn't she just say, Jay is here. Are you dressed yet? Sometimes Daddy would do the same thing when he was referring to Jay. I didn't like it, but I just kept it to myself.

Anyway I slipped on my shoes and grabbed my purse. "Yes Ma, I'm dressed, and I'm coming out." When I got into the living room, my whole family was standing around looking at Jay. No one had invited him in or even offered him a seat. They just stared at him. When I walked out front, I was glad to see Jay's smiling face.

He said, "Hi," and told me how nice I looked. I smiled and told Mama that we were leaving. Jay and I walked out the door and down the steps. When we got into the car, Jay had gotten some eight-track tapes together. We always liked listening to music when we drove around.

When I looked up, I noticed Daddy standing on the porch, at the door. Jay waved at him, but it looked like Daddy wanted to talk all night. "Nice tires you got there." The car belonged to Jay's uncle. It was olive green with big, white- wall tires and an antenna on the back.

"Thank you, Sir." I told Jay to start the car, because next, Daddy would be outside.

"You don't see cars that look like that down here much."

I knew then that it was time to go. I looked across Jay's shoulders and waved goodbye to Daddy, and Jay pulled away and put an eight-track in. The first song that came on was by the Delfonics, "La-la Means I Love You." Jay always entertained me by singing along with the record when he knew that I liked the song. And it made me feel special.

When we got to the drive-in movie, Jay parked the car. He turned the radio to the station that was used to get the sound that we needed to hear the movie. Then he got out of the car to get hot dogs and drinks. I wanted to hear some music until he got back. While I was scanning the radio dial trying to find WMBM, I heard Barbara Mason singing "Yes, I'm Ready." I sang along with her. I loved that song. I turned the radio back to the station that Jay had it on when I saw him coming back to the car, but I was in the mood for love.

When Jay got into the car, he must have felt my mood. I was not interested in the movie, and neither was he. We put the food down on the front seat and the drinks on the floor. Then Jay suggested that we get in the back seat, so that we could relax better. I opened the door and got into the back seat. Jay pulled me closer to him and kissed me. I kissed him back. We had never been alone in that kind of a situation before, and I didn't know what to do. But Jay did. He kissed me and touched me in places I didn't know could bring so much pleasure. I had feelings that I never knew existed. When Walter and I were dating, we kissed and necked and sometimes our bodies would be so close that not even a beam of sunlight could get between us. But the chemistry just hadn't been there.

Anyway Jay continued to kiss me. As he whispered sweet nothings in my ear, my body was floating into space, while I tried to collect my mind, which was not an easy job. Everything seemed to be getting out of control, but I managed to get a handle on the situation. Without a warning, I was in Jay's arms one minute, and the next I was in the front seat.

When I looked in the back seat again, Jay had one arm on the back of the seat and the other in the air. I had to laugh because I'd jumped in the front as if the back seat was on fire. Jay got back in the front seat too. He looked at me as if he didn't know what to say, and neither did I. He put his hand on my shoulder and squeezed it. I put a hot dog in my mouth and turned my head to the movie screen. I didn't want to talk, touch, kiss or anything. I kept thinking about what had just happened or almost happened in the back seat. I could tell that Jay wanted to talk by the way he looked at me.

"Louise, was I taking things too fast for you? Did I frighten you?" Jay asked with an apologetic look on his face. I wanted to say, Hell, yeah. Now take me home. But I was a big girl, so I had to act grown up.

"No, you didn't frighten me, I'm cool." I lied.

"Babe, please know that I'd never do anything that you didn't want me to do. OK?" Jay took me in his arms and just held me for awhile. I began to feel uncomfortable. He was looking at me as if I had V-I-R-G-I-N written across my forehead. Then he asked the big question. what to say.

I thought about what my friend Sandy had said, and I thought being a virgin was not a good thing, but I finally answered Jay. "Yes, Jay. I'm a virgin. So what? What do you have to say about that?" At that point I was angry and ready to go home.

"I'd say that I'm proud that my girl is a virgin, and that I love you." Sandy had lied again. She'd told me that they'd leave you once they found out that you were a virgin. I smiled at Jay and he smiled back. We took our drinks from the cardboard box and looked at the movie screen again, but the movie was over. Everyone was starting up their cars and leaving. We had not seen any of the movie. We laughed about it because neither one of us had ever seen the movie, and we had no clue of what it was about. We only knew the title.

It was nine o'clock, and we still had more time to be together. We wanted to spend as much time together as we could, whenever we got the chance. Jay would be leaving for Detroit soon, and I didn't know when I'd see him again. Jay suggested that we go for a ride, and maybe we could drop by his house. If his mother was at home, he'd introduce us to each other. That idea kind of shook me up a little. I felt sort of nervous about meeting Jay's mom. So I asked him, "Does your mother ever ask about me?" I wanted to know.

"Yeah, she asks about you whenever I'm getting dressed to go pick you up. "Well, what does she ask you about me?"

"She wants to know when I'm going to invite you over."

"And you said ... .?" I had to drag every word out of Jay that night.

"OK, Louise. Enough with the third degree. I'll let you meet her tonight."

"Jay, I'm kind of nervous. Maybe I'll meet her another time."

"No. Please Louise, come with me to the house tonight. I want you to meet my mom. If she's still there, she's going to ask you to dinner on Sunday. Will you come?"

"So, you really have been discussing me with your mom?" It made me feel good that Jay and his mom had been talking about me, and had already decided to invite me to dinner. "Sure, I'd love to meet your mom, but I'll have to ask my mom and dad first."

"Oh! Yeah. You can meet my uncle too. I know he'll be there, because we have his car."

"Were you and your uncle talking about me too?" I gave Jay a look that said (and don't lie). He looked back at me with that crooked smile, and I knew that he was thinking something dirty. I playfully socked Jay on the shoulder, and then he answered.

Still smiling he said, "Yeah we talked about you." "And what did you two talk about?"

"I told my uncle how much I love you, and that I'm proud to be your man." "And what did your uncle say about that?"

"He said that he could hardly wait to meet you."

And I could hardly wait to meet him; I wanted to see what kind of a person would buy a car that looked like the one we had been riding around in. I looked at my watch, and it was ten o'clock. Jay had just pulled up in front of the house. I felt nervous again. I considered asking Jay to just keep going, but I thought against it. Once we'd parked, we could see Jay's uncle sitting on the porch having a drink. The Hennessey bottle was almost empty, and he was pouring himself yet another drink. He was dressed in a green silk suit, a gold silk shirt, with his chest opened, green gators, green socks, and a hat with a gold feather on the side of it. My mouth fell open. Jay was laughing at the look on my face as I checked his uncle out.

"What's the matter Louise?" "Your uncle ... why so formal?"

"Uncle Jim dresses like that all of the time. He's a ladies man." "And what does that mean?" I asked.

"I'll tell you all about it later."

I later learned that Jay's uncle was a pimp. Jim lived in Detroit with his brother Lenny. They owned a night club together. Jim's street name was Diamond Jim. Jim knew and was friends with all of the drug dealers, hustlers, other pimps and junkies on the streets. He was known for wearing gold or green silk suits, a diamond necklace and a diamond bracelet that spelled J-I-M, and he wore a "J" made of diamonds on each pinky finger. Jim was not only a pimp, he was a junky. That's why his brother Lenny wanted Jay to keep up with the money, once he knew that his health was failing.

While we were talking, Jim had noticed that we were parked outside, and he was coming to the car. He came around to my side and opened the door for me. He reached for my hand, helped me out, closed the door behind me, and then kissed my hand. Jay introduced us. "Louise, this is my uncle Jim."

"Hi, Jim," I said.

"Jim, this is my lady, Louise."

"Hello, Young Lady, it's a pleasure to meet you." We walked into the house.

Jay invited me into the living room to have a seat. "Jim, where is Ma?" Jay asked.

"Your mother was called into work about an hour ago, Slim." Jim went to the cabinet and pulled out another bottle of Hennessey. He offered Jay a drink, but Jay waved the glass away.

Then he offered me a glass of soda pop, but I said, "No thanks." Jay had wandered off to another part of the house. I didn't know what pimps talked about, so I said nothing. I didn't fully understand what a pimp was or did.

Jim must have known that I was sort of nervous. He came over and sat across from me shaking the ice in his glass of Hennessey and smiled. Then he said, "I guess Slim told you that we'll be leaving for Detroit soon."

"Yes, Sir, he just never gave me an exact day." I looked around for Jay, but he had gone into one of the other rooms. I could tell that Jim was getting tipsy.

He told me not to call him, Sir. "I'm Diamond Jim," he said loudly, and when he raised his glass of Hennessey up in the air, it spilled all over the sleeve of his green silk suit. Then the door bell rang. Jim put the glass that he was drinking from down on the coffee table and answered the door. "Who is it?" Jim called out, as he wiped the stain from his suit.

"It's me, Lisa, and my friend; we met you at the corner store today." Jim opened the door and let Lisa and her friend inside just as Jay walked out of one of the back rooms.

"Jim, who's at the door?"

"It's OK. I've got it, Slim. Just two of my women. They're taking me out tonight." Jim was drunk. He didn't bother to change, and he'd wasted his drink on his suit. The Hennessey had dried, but the stain was still there, and Jim didn't seem to mind.

"Bye Jim. Nice meeting you." "Oh, yeah. It's Louise, isn't it?"

"Yes, Sir," I answered. The expression on Jim's face told me that I'd said the wrong thing.

"Please don't call me, Sir. I'm Diamond Jim." Then he left with the two young girls that were almost my age. I looked at Jay. He smiled.

"Jay, she couldn't be more than seventeen." I said. "I know."

"But Jim is old enough to be her father."

"I know," Jay said again, as he took my hand and led me into a room that looked like it belonged to him and his brother. I could tell which side of the room belonged to Jay. He had all kinds of newspaper clippings, pamphlets, and all sorts of information about the Black Panthers pinned on the walls and all over the tables. I was looking for a picture of another girl on his dresser or table, but I saw none.

"So where did you hide it?" "Hide what?"

"Where did you hide her picture? That's what you were doing back here while I was up front with that nut, isn't it?"

"No, I wanted to clear away some of the junk before I brought you back here to hang out with me. You are my only girl." At that moment I realized that Jay had cleared off the bed. He wanted us to hang out on the bed, in his room, with no one else home. I felt nervous again. I wanted to talk about the Black Panthers.

"Jay, did you ever consider joining the Black Panthers?" "Yeah."
"Well, what happened?"

"Louise, let's not talk about the Black Panthers tonight. Babe, we need to talk about us. We have so little time left together before I'll be leaving for Detroit."

"Exactly when are you leaving, Jay?" "We'll be leaving on Monday morning."

"Oh, no. Jay, I hate to think of how much I'm going to miss you." "I'm going to miss you too, Babe."

We kicked off our shoes and lay across the bed. Jay rolled me over into his arms and kissed me. I closed my eyes and tried to think of all Daddy's Rules, but I was so turned on I couldn't keep a thought in my head. I got that tingling feeling all over my body again. When I opened my eyes, Jay's brown eyes were looking right into mine. Then he asked, "Louise are you really ready to love me the way I want you to?"

Part of me wanted to say, yes, and the other part was afraid to answer. I didn't know what to do. I got nervous again, so I sat up and put my shoes back on my feet and began to stand up. Jay took my hand and held onto it. He stood up too. "Louise wait. Don't panic. Nothing will ever happen with us if you don't want it to. OK, Babe? I love you, and I'd never hurt you." I began to feel relaxed again. We sat on the bed again, and Jay kissed me.

I thought about the way I'd reacted to Jay's question and how fast Jay read my body language. I started to laugh. Jay's thoughts were the same. He began to laugh too. I kicked my shoes back off, and Jay turned the radio on and closed the door. I wished he had not shut the door as I was still a little nervous. But I managed to get past the panic. Jay walked back to the bed, and he lay down next to me. We relaxed again and started to talk. Jay told me that they were leaving Monday morning, and that he really wanted me to have Sunday dinner with him and his family. We talked about his sister Joy and how outgoing she was, his brother Gene, who was a pot head, and his mother and how she was in denial of their dysfunctional family. Jay said that his step father was just a living soul who lived at that residence. We laughed and agreed that most families were dysfunctional.

I was really relaxed, and I wanted a cool drink. Jay went into the kitchen to get one for both of us, and I went into the bathroom to check my hair and makeup. When I re-entered the room, Jay seem to be setting the scene for seduction. He'd taken off his shirt. He then suggested that I take my blouse off, so that it didn't get wrinkled. But I said no and sat on the bed. Jay ran his fingers across the top of my blouse and pulled it back to show my breast and stopped. The radio was on and the Intruders were singing a song that we both loved, "Cowboys and Girls." We snapped our fingers, danced and sang along with the music. We were having big fun. When the song finished, we flopped across the bed. Jay pulled me into his arms and kissed me again.

"I love you so much, Babe."

"I love you too, Jay." I admitted. The look on Jay's face, and the tone of his voice made me realize that things were getting serious. "What's the matter, Jay? Why are you looking so serious?" I asked.

"I'm OK, don't let it bother you, Babe. I just . ...." "You just what, Jay?"

"I just want you so bad, but I don't want to pressure you. You know?" I didn't. I didn't even know what to say, so I kissed him, and that was like throwing gas on a fire. Jay kissed me back, but very slowly, making sure that I understood the effect I had on him. I felt it alright, I was on cloud nine; I thought I saw the moon. I tried to take control of the situation by trying to push Jay off of me, but I was too weak. We explored each other's mouth licking and sucking each others lips. I liked the way Jay slid his hand up and down my bare back; I was in ecstasy.

Then Jay knew it was time to take control. He was down to his boxers when we heard someone open and close the front door. We jumped up from the bed. Jay scrambled to find his clothes. He found his pants, put them on and walked out into the living room. He didn't bother to put on his shoes or shirt. But I needed to put on some clothes. In our moment of passion the sensation was so intense, I couldn't even remember when or how we got undressed.

I could still hear voices in the living room, but with my head still spinning, I managed to get my skirt and my under garments back on. I began to try to clean things up and straighten up the bed, and then get myself together. When Jay came back in the room, I was coming out of the bathroom. "Who was it, Jay?" I asked.

"It was Jim, he came back to change clothes." I could hear the door close, and Jim was gone.

"It's almost eleven o'clock, we'd better leave now," I reminded Jay.

"OK, I'll put my shoes and shirt back on, and then we can leave whenever you are ready. I reached in my purse and got my comb, because my afro was still flat on one side. I could just imagine Mama's reaction if she saw me coming in looking like that. We finished getting dressed and checked each other out, then rushed out to the car. It was eleven-fifteen, and I had to be home by twelve.

As Jay drove me home, the car was silent. The radio was off, and you could hear nothing but the wind coming through the window. I don't know what Jay was thinking about, but I was having flashbacks and wondering what would have happened if Jim would not have come back to the house. Jay finally turned on the radio, and I heard a female vocalist. She was singing a tune called, "Tonight is The Night." It was very catchy, and it had a good beat to it. I could almost sing along with her. When the song was over, the DJ announced that we'd just heard Miami's own Betty Wright. While the song was playing and I was singing, I realized that she could have been singing about me.

Jay reached over and took hold of my hand. He exited the expressway and stopped at the light. Then he kissed my hand. It was almost like communicating without talking. Jay put my hand on his chest, and I moved closer to him. Then he put his arm around me, and my body went limp and I melted into his arms.

As we turned onto my street, Jay asked me if I'd be able to have dinner with him and his family the next day, which was Sunday. "I don't know," I answered.

"Why?" Jay asked.

"If we get home on time tonight, it's possible," I answered. "Do you want me to ask your parents or should you?"

"I'll ask them," I said.

"Call me and let me know what time to pick you up."

"OK." Jay parked the car and walked around to open my door. I could see two guys coming toward us. The street lamps didn't let me get a good look at them at first. As they got closer, I recognized them. It was Walter and his friend. I had not talked to Walter since I had broken it off with him months ago. I stepped out of the car. Jay and I started up the walkway to my house. Walter slowed down to speak, "Hi Louise, long time, no see." he said, smiling more than he needed to. I could see that he had been drinking.

"Hi guys, this is Jay. Look, we're in a hurry, so good night." I could see that Walter was looking for trouble, and Jay wasn't having it.

"No, don't try to rush in now. You shouldn't have let your man keep you out all night."

Well, that pissed Jay off. "Man, get the fu— on down the street." Walter flipped Jay off. Then Jay walked back around the car and punched Walter in the mouth. He went down holding his hand in front of his mouth. I screamed, and the front door flew open. Walter's friend helped him get up, and they ran down the street.

"What happened out here?" Daddy demanded.

"It's OK now, Sir. Those two clowns tried to pick a fight with your daughter.

They were trying to disrespect her, but I wasn't going to have it."

I told Daddy that it was all Walter's fault, and that he had tried to cause problems.

"Ya'll have a fight?"

"No Sir. I punched him, and he went down, Sir." "And he got up and ran," I added.

"OK, Louise. Go in the house now. See you later, Son. And thanks." Daddy just dismissed us both, didn't even give us a chance to say goodnight, but he did tell Jay thanks. Although I wondered if Daddy was saying thanks for punching Walter in the mouth, or thanks for defending my honor.

Jay called me the next day. I could hear the uncertainty in his voice. "Hello Babe. I hope you are not mad because I punched that guy last night."

"Oh, no, Jay. I'm not mad. He got just what he deserved. He was just showing off in front of his friend."

"I know I was wrong, but I let my jealousy go to my head. Then I clicked. I didn't make trouble for you, did I?"

"No, you didn't cause any trouble. Jay, were you really jealous?"

"Yeah! I was jealous. I could tell he was your Ex, and he couldn't stand the fact that I was out with you. I could imagine the sh— that went through his head. That's why he tried to disrespect you. But you are my girl, and I couldn't have that."

Jay really did love me; he was jealous! He was letting me know how much he cared—just the way I had imagined love should be.

"What about dinner today? Did you ask them yet?" "Yes, Jay, I asked them, and it's OK."

"Good, I'll pick you up at five."

"OK, but I'll have to get back by nine. I have school tomorrow." "OK, Babe. See you at five. Love you."

"Love you too. Bye." We hung up the phone. Just hearing Jay's voice made me have flashbacks from the night before. All I could think about was what almost happened, and did I really want it to happen again.

It was almost four o'clock, and Jay would be picking me up at five. I went to the closet to find something to wear. There wasn't much to choose from, and I wanted to find something Jay's mother would approve of. I wanted to make a good impression. Everything was running through my head, but I managed to calm myself down. I showered and started to get dressed.

Four-fifty and Jay was knocking on the door. Daddy opened the door and let Jay in. They shook hands, and Daddy showed him in and closed the door.

CHAPTER 8

Sunday Dinner at Ms. Lynn's

"Good evening, Mr. Robert." "Hi Son, how you doing?" "Just fine, Sir. I want to apologize for the disturbance in front of your house last night."

"No problem, Son. I always knew that guy was a trouble maker." I could hear them talking in the living room as I hurried to get dressed. "How long will you and your uncle be here?"

"We will be leaving in the morning, Sir."

"Hope ya'll have a safe trip. I'll get Louise for you." I was glad Daddy didn't go on and on about how he always knew Walter was no good for me. I finished getting ready as fast as I could and joined them in the living room. When I walked out, the first thing I saw was Jay's welcoming smile. I took his hand, and he kissed me on the cheek while Daddy was standing right there. I held my breath because I didn't know what Daddy's reaction was going to be. But Daddy just looked at me and smiled, and I smiled back. But in my head I was thinking, if Daddy only knew how Jay kissed me last night, he wouldn't be smiling like that! We said goodnight to everyone. Jay opened the door, and we left.

We got into the car, and Jay drove toward the expressway. Jay lived about five miles from my house, which gave us plenty of time to talk. He filled me in on his family again. He said he wanted me to know what I was going to run into. We laughed and agreed that we both had dysfunctional families. When we drove up to Jay's house, I could tell everyone was home by all the cars parked in the yard. We got out of the car and started up the walkway, and we could hear someone crying. I could see Lisa on the screened porch, and she was still crying when Jay opened the door.

Diamond Jim had been going out with Lisa while he was visiting Miami, and sometimes Diamond Jim would go out with Lisa and her friend together. That freaks, if you ask me. Lisa said that Diamond Jim promised to take her back to Detroit whenever they went. Lisa was a young lady who grew up on the streets of Opa-Locka. From age thirteen on, Lisa's stepfather had abused her sexually. Her mother put her out of the house, because she refused to believe Lisa when she told her what her stepfather was doing to her. Her mother had been in another room sleeping off the drugs and alcohol the stepfather had given her.

When Lisa's stepfather found out that her mother had put her out of the house, they had a terrible fight that turned deadly. He beat her about the head with a lead pipe, and during the fight Lisa's mother shot him to death in their kitchen. Her mother died two days later in the hospital. Lisa lived with her cousins where she found more abuse, so she ran away and began living with anyone who'd let her stay the night. Jay said he thought Lisa's mother put her out to keep her stepfather away from her, and that society made Lisa the person she was.

Lisa's mind was set on going with Diamond Jim, and he was pleading with her to stay until he sent for her. But Lisa didn't want to hear it. Jay kept explaining to me that he knew nothing of what Jim had done. Then he turned to Jim and asked him, "Jim, Man, what's going on?"

"Yeah, Man, I told this girl that I was going to take her to Detroit so that she could work for me, and she got the wrong idea. And now I'm trying to tell her what the deal is, but she doesn't want to hear it." Lisa started to cry louder. Jay's mother rushed out to the porch to see what had happened. His stepfather was right behind her. Lisa stopped crying for a moment, and Jay's mother asked me into the house. I wanted to find out about Lisa, but I managed to turn my attention to Jay's parents. We stepped into the living room, and they introduced themselves.

"Hello, Louise. I'm Jay's mother, Ms. Lynn, and this is my husband, Mr. Connie." I greeted them both with a smile. Jay's mother seated me on the couch, next to her, and told me to call her Ms. Lynn. I looked around for Jay. I could hear him and his stepfather telling Jim to take Lisa home, or wherever he wanted to take her, but to get her out of the house. Ms. Lynn wanted to know all about my family, how old I was, and where I went to school.

As we talked, Jay's brother came out of the room smiling, and very slowly he said, "Hi Louise, I'm Jay's brother." His clothes smelled like he'd been smoking pot; his eyes were red and glazed. I looked at Ms. Lynn and then back into his red eyes and said, "Hi," to him. Then he turned around very slowly and said, "Oh, yeah, my name is Gene." I smiled and looked at Ms. Lynn again, but she didn't seem to think anything was wrong with that picture. Then I knew what Jay was talking about when he said that Ms. Lynn was in denial. She just excused herself, and said that she had to finish her dinner. I amused myself looking at pictures around the living room while I waited for Jay to come back into the house. When he finally returned, we sat on the couch and talked about what we were going to do after dinner.

We heard the front door slam, and Joy came in. She had been to a party the night before and had spent the night with her friend Pam. Pam's house was the place to go when you wanted to sleep over, have a party, leave home, or just watch TV. It was always alright with Pam's mom. She was a single mom and loved to have Pam's friends around. When Joy saw me, she hurried over and gave me a big hug. I could smell the alcohol on her breath. She had been drinking, and her clothes smelled like smoke. "Joy have you been drinking?" I whispered. She tried to whisper back, but the alcohol was still taking its toll on her. She had no idea how loud she was talking.

"No … not drinking. The punch was spiked last night."

Jay heard her and blurted out, "No, Joy. You've been drinking. Don't even try that spiked punch routine."

Before I could ask her about the smoke, she pulled out a pack of Kools and lit one up. My mouth flew open, and I couldn't believe it. Joy was fifteen and was smoking. Jay told Joy the pro's and con's of drinking when she went out to parties and what could happen to her. I noticed Joy, as Jay talked to her about drinking. She looked tired, and her eyes were red and puffy. She looked like a forty year-old in the body of a twenty year-old. Joy was really developed for her age; she had curves I'd only hoped for. "What do your parents say about you smoking?" I asked.

"They used to get upset, but now they say I have to support my own habits. "No, they buy them for her, but they say that the money is for her lunch money,' Jay added.

Ms. Lynn came into the living room to tell everyone that dinner was ready. We all went into the dining room, and Ms. Lynn directed us to our seats. The meal was well prepared and tasty. Ms. Lynn served baked chicken, green beans, macaroni and cheese, and yams, with sweet tea to drink. All of my favorites. While we were eating, Ms. Lynn invited me to dinner the following Sunday. I accepted the invitation. I looked at Jay; he seemed to be pleased and so was Joy. Ms. Lynn said that she would have Joy call me and confirm. I said, "OK." Joy said that she'd call me that Friday, and that maybe we could hangout together. When she said hangout together, I knew I'd need a rain check, but I just smiled and said, "OK."

Their brother Gene started to laugh. Jay asked him what was so funny. Gene just shook his head and pointed at Joy. I could see an evil frown come across Joy's face. Then she set her ice tea down and asked Gene, "What are you laughing about stupid?" You still high or what?" If looks could kill, the daggers in Joy's eyes would have ripped Gene apart. Gene didn't even acknowledge Joy's insults or name calling.

In slow motion, Gene looked at Jay, scratched his beard and said, "Man, I'm telling you. Don't let your lady start running around with Joy and her crowd. The places that she goes are rough. You just might loose your lady." Gene laughed again and stuffed some more chicken in his mouth. I could see by his body language that Jay was offended.

"Man, I'm not worried about Louise. She knows what she wants, and she can take care of herself."

Jay was upset with Gene. When I looked into Jay's eyes, I read, "Let's Go," all over Jay's face. He got up from the table, and I followed him. Then he asked me to wait for him on the porch because he wanted to get some eight-tracks; we were going to sit in the car and listen to some music. Jim had left his car, and he had driven Lisa's friend's car back to the hotel. I could still hear them fussing back at the dining room table. Gene was telling Ms. Lynn that she didn't know Joy like he did, when she's out of the house. He said that they were in denial when it came to Joy's behavior. "No Gene, we don't know Joy when she's out of the house. Why don't you tell us?" Ms. Lynn demanded. My ears were like two radio receivers, I wanted to know what Joy was doing when she was out of the house too.

Jay came out of the room with the eight-tracks, and we went outside and got into the car. Jay and I wanted to spend as much time as we could together because Jay was leaving the next day and going back to Detroit. We sat in the car, feeling the breeze blow across our faces from the palm trees waving in the front yard. The day had been hot, and the humidity was at its peak. We welcomed the breeze. Jay popped in an eight-track tape. We loved our music. Some of the songs that we listened to played a special part in our relationship.

The songs just seemed to say the words that we couldn't think of to say to each other. Jay turned the music up and the Impressions were singing, "I'm So Proud." Jay sang along with them. He liked singing to me, and I liked watching him perform for me. We listened to The Dells, The Temptations, and Smokey. I thought that day couldn't get any better. We were laughing, singing and enjoying the moment. After awhile we noticed that everyone inside, had come outside, and had taken a seat on the front porch to watch us. Jay cranked the car up, backed out and drove off.

"Jay, why did you do that? I didn't say goodbye."

"I'll say all of your goodbyes for you when I get back." "Jay, what's wrong?" I asked, not understanding his mood.

'I only have two hours to spend with you today. I have to leave tomorrow, and I want you all to myself today, without having the "Odd Squad" watching me. I loved it when Jay wanted all of my attention. We drove around for about ten minuets, and no one said a thing. Now, what's wrong, I wondered? Finally we stopped in front of a motel. Jay parked the car and just looked straight ahead, not saying a word. Then he popped in another tape.

"Why are we stopping here, Jay?" I already knew what Jay had in mind.

"I just thought that we could relax a little better here, you know just talk or watch TV or whatever you want to do."

"And that's it, huh?"

"Louise, I know what you are thinking, but I just wanted a little quiet time with you. That's all," he pleaded.

"OK, we do need to talk, and we do need some time together. Let's go in." I wanted to be alone with Jay anyway, but I wasn't sure what I wanted to do. I knew that sex was in the picture somewhere, but I didn't know if I really wanted it.

We got out of the car and walked up to the motel. Jay pulled out a key with a big number 72 on it. He already had a key! I stopped and looked at Jay ... he wanted to smile but tried to hide it. He knew it was a touchy situation, and he didn't want to push it. We got inside the room. I stood by the door with my arms folded and demanded, "Jay, why do you already have a key to this door? When did you plan this?"

"Louise, I just thought that you would want us to be alone like this since this is our last night together before I have to leave."

"It's OK, you're right. I do want to be alone with you."

"Babe, you don't have to do anything you don't want to do." I laughed to myself because every time Jay said, 'Babe, you don't have to do anything you don't want to do,' I knew what he wanted to do. He was just trying to get me to relax.

I looked around the room at the floral-green curtains that matched the bed spread, a small end table with a green lamp next to the bed, and a clean tile floor with a throw rug that matched the bed spread. The bathroom was clean and had the smell of Pine-Sol. I came out of the bathroom to tell Jay that I was satisfied with the room, and he'd already taken off his pants. "Jay what are you doing?" I asked.

"Oh, yeah. We need to take off our clothes so they don't get wrinkled." Jay's answer made sense, but it didn't take much of an explanation to convince me. I had already made up my mind what I wanted to do that night. But I didn't want Jay to think it was that easy to get my clothes off, so I thought I'd give him a hard time for awhile.

"Who said anything about lying down? I can't get my clothes wrinkled sitting here on the bed talking, now can I, Jay?"

"No, not if we just sit. I just thought you wanted to relax?"

"Let's just sit here and talk," I said, but we couldn't think of anything to say at the moment. I got up and changed the channel. The TV only had three channels 4, 7, and10, and nothing interesting was on. So Jay turned the sound on the TV down, and he turned the radio on.

"Jay, see if you can get WAME?" I asked. He finally got it. "Hey! That's the song you like, Babe."

"Oh, yeah! That's Betty Wright singing "Yes, I'm Ready." I began to sing along with Betty, and realizing how off beat I was sounding, I started to laugh. I was feeling more relaxed. I looked at my watch, and it was already eight o'clock. I wanted to get close and personal with Jay, so I had him unzip my dress. Jay's smile lit up his face. He unzipped me and helped me take my dress off. He even hung it up for me. I sat on the side of the bed; Jay sat next to me and kissed me on the cheek.

"What the matter, Louise? You look so sad."

"I just wish you could stay a little while longer, Jay. After tonight you'll be gone."

"I know Louise. That's why tonight is so special. When we get lonely or start to miss each other, we'll have tonight to remember. I wish that I could stay longer too, but you know what I have to do."

"I know, I know. It's The Club."

"Yeah, it's The Club. You see how Jim is. He puts a lot of stress on Lenny. Sometimes I have to watch Jim when he gets so tied up with his women, and he's not watching what is going on in The Club." I was sick of talking about Diamond Jim and his women. I was already upset that Jay had to go back to Detroit because of Jim. I didn't even want to hear his name anymore. I started to cry. "Louise, please don't cry?"

"Jay, I'm going to miss you so much."

"I'll miss you too, Babe. I'll be thinking about you day and night." "I really am glad we got together like this."

"Louise, let's make this a night to remember. We'll only go as far as you want things to go. OK?" There he goes again, I thought.

But the way Jay kissed me, and the sensation it gave me, made me want to go as far as he wanted to go. My body felt warm and started to tingle again. I pushed Jay off of me until I could get control of the situation and was able to think again. I hated it when I lost control of my mind like that. Then Jay lay on top of me and held down both of my hands, and he said, "Louise, just relax. Stop trying to control everything. We love each other. Just let your feelings flow. Jay kissed me again and again until I was relaxed and until I surrendered myself to him. I felt pain before pleasure with a sensation I'd never felt before or even knew existed.

When it was over, Jay held me in his arms until I was calmer. I wanted to sleep, but Jay said that we were running late, and we had to get home on time that night. I rushed into the bathroom and washed myself up as best I could. As I checked my hair and make-up, I kept thinking, what is supposed to happen next? What do I do or say to Jay? After all, it was the first time I'd ever done anything like that before. When I opened the bathroom door, Jay was sitting on the bed smiling and looking right at me. I didn't know whether to smile or cry. I'd had sex with him, and the next day he'd be thousands of miles away from me. I thought, will tonight's memories haunt me or delight me after he's gone? I began to feel confused. "Babe, are you alright?"

"I don't know. I guess I'm OK." "Did I hurt you? If I did, I'm sorry."

"No, no. You didn't. Let's go, I want to go home," I insisted. I couldn't look at Jay. I don't know why, but I just couldn't.

We got into the car, and still no one said anything. Jay backed out of the parking space and drove about five minutes down the street and onto the expressway. Still no one said a word. We drove on the expressway until it was time to exit and turn onto my street, and we still were not talking. When Jay parked the car in front of my house, I got out without saying a word or even waiting for Jay to walk with me. I rushed to the door, knocked, and Daddy opened it for me. He and Mama checked me out from head to toe. Then I got the look of approval.

"Everything OK, Louise?"

"Yeah, Daddy. Everything is fine."

"You had a good dinner?" Mama asked.

"Yeah, the dinner was great, and I met Jay's whole family." I just wanted to go in my room, get a hot shower and go to bed.

"What did she cook?" Mama asked. The door bell rang. As Daddy went to answer it, someone knocked really hard. I looked at Mama, and we followed Daddy to the door. When Daddy opened the door, it was Jay standing there looking sad.

"Mr. Robert, may I talk to Louise?" Mama and Daddy looked at me, smiled and said goodnight.

"What happened, Jay?" I asked.

"What happened? Louise, if I've hurt you, or if I've done something wrong, please tell me. You just jumped out of the car, no kiss, no goodnight, nothing. You tell me what's wrong? Please."

"I'm sorry, Jay. So much has happened so fast. I don't know how to act or what to say. You know I've never had that experience before. What we did tonight was the first for me." Jay looked around to see if Daddy had really gone to bed. He put his hand to my mouth.

"Sh-sh-sh, Louise. Don't talk so loud. I understand what you are saying, but I just couldn't leave things like that. Tonight was too special for both of us not to even say our last goodbyes the way we should." Jay whispered.

"Jay, you must have thought I had lost my mind, the way I jumped out of the car and rushed into the house." Jay kept telling me to talk softer or even to whisper. Jay said that he didn't want Daddy to hear what we were talking about, and he didn't want to get beat down for loving one of Daddy's little girls. We laughed about it. Then we walked out to the porch and had our last kisses and goodbyes. Jay left, and I locked the door behind him.

CHAPTER 9

Friends

It had been a night I'd never forget. I walked into the bedroom I shared with my sister Bobbie, and she was still up. I wondered if she was really preparing her things for the next day or was she waiting up for me, so that she could find out about my date. I went to the dresser to get some night clothes and to get ready for my shower. Then I realized that I'd been standing in the same spot for awhile, as if I was in a trance. I could hear Bobbie calling me, "Louise, what's wrong with you?"

"Nothing, why?"

"You've been standing there like you've got something on your mind." "I'm OK."

I wondered if she could tell Jay and I'd had sex that night? But how could she tell when Mama and Daddy couldn't tell? I was just nervous. I wished Bobbie and I were closer. I needed someone to talk to, a sister to share secrets with, and a sister to tell me what to do after experiencing what I had that night. I needed a big sister to comfort me. Bobbie had already figured out that something had happened on my date by the way I'd been acting. She'd already asked me if something was on my mind. I wondered if she was really concerned, or if she was trying to set me up to tell her something so she could run back and tell Daddy. I didn't want to fight with her; I couldn't handle it that night.

"Bobbie, I don't want to fight. So please, just leave me alone."

"I know, I don't want to fight either, Louise. I just want you to know that you can talk to me, if you want. I know that you don't trust me, and I can't blame you, the way we've been fighting this past year."

"You've got that right," I answered.

"You see, Louise, I have an idea of what happened tonight."

"Well, I've got an idea of what's going to happen if you don't get out of my face."

Bobbie ignored my anger and sat on my bed. She looked sincere when she said, "Louise, it's already happened to me. Rico and I have had sex, and I had no one to talk to. I know what you're feeling. I'm here for you if you want to talk."

My sister was reaching out to me at a time when I needed her more than ever. I began to cry. She gave me her shoulder to cry on, and I was glad. It was indeed time for us to get past our issues. I dried my eyes and gave my sister a big hug. I wasn't ready to talk yet, but I told her that we'd talk later. I got my night clothes and went into the bathroom. Bobbie came to the bathroom door and asked if I was going to take a shower. "Yeah, I'm going to take a shower, why?"

"Don't take a shower," she said. "You need to get in the tub and soak. You'll feel better in the morning." I got in the tub like she suggested. It was a little painful, but it made me feel better. Every time I'd move around in the tub, the discomfort gave me flashbacks of what had happened in the motel room with Jay, and yet, it made me smile. When I got out of the tub and went back into our room, Bobbie and I smiled at each other. We were glad we were talking and hopefully would be closer than we had been. I tried to make conversation with her since we were talking.

"I see that you and Rico are still hanging in there. You seem to be very happy."

"Yeah, I'm happy with him. We've been together for a year now."

"That's great. Well, I'd better try and get some sleep. Good night."

"You won't get any sleep tonight, Sister. Those flashbacks are going to play out over and over in your head." I knew she was right. I started smiling, and then we both started laughing. When I realized we were laughing together, it felt good. I closed my eyes and hoped for some sleep. But sleep didn't come easy. Everytime I closed my eyes, I had flashbacks of everything that happened in that motel room.

I got up early the next morning. I'd only gotten about an hour of sleep. I wanted to walk to school alone and just think and have flashbacks as much as I wanted to, without anyone looking at me strangely. I was really trying to avoid my friend Sandy. I wasn't ready to share my glorious weekend with anyone just yet.

CHAPTER 10

The Day After

After I got to school, my first three classes were a total waste. I didn't even know what was going on. All I could think of was sleeping with Jay the night before—it played itself out over and over. Then I thought about how Jay was gone, and so was my virginity. I was ready to burst into tears when the bell rang for lunch. I slowly walked out of the building and across the street. The Royal Castle looked sort of empty, so I went in and got a booth by the window. Jay was gone, and I didn't want to talk to anyone else. I gazed across the street, and I watched my classmates buzz in and out of the soda shop. It was always full. I thought about how things would be now that my sister and I were talking again, especially since Jay was gone. Now I had someone to talk to. I wondered if Jay was thinking of me too and having flashbacks like I was. Then I went over to the counter and ordered some fries and a drink and went back to my booth.

As I slid in to sit closer to the window, someone slid in beside me, and kissed me on the cheek. When I turned around, it was Jay! I was so happy I started to cry. I thought it would be at least a year before I'd see him again. But here he was, sitting by me saying, "I love you," to me. I couldn't control my tears. When I was finally able to talk, I wanted to know what had happened. "I thought you and Jim left this morning," I said.

"Babe, you know I couldn't leave Dade County without a kiss from you." "Jay, I'm so glad you are here. I was missing you already."

"I know. I watched you from the doorway—you looked so sad."

"Whenever I'm missing you, I'll have last night to keep me holding on, and when you hear our song, "La-La Means I love you," remember me. Jay and I talked for a little while. Then I could see Diamond Jim waving for Jay to come on, and at the same time we heard the school bell ring. We kissed and said our last good-byes. As Jay walked me out, I noticed some of my classmates standing around watching our little emotional scene. When Jay got into the car, he waved and said, "La-La, Babe," and I said, "Take care my love," still crying on the inside. The walk across the street seemed to take forever, and I could hardly pick up one foot and put it in front of the other.

When I got back to school, I walked into my classroom, and I saw someone I didn't want to talk to, my friend Sandy. She had already talked to Walter and gotten another version of what had happened on that Saturday night. Then I told her what really happened, and we had a good laugh about it. Walter had told everyone that he'd beaten Jay up, and that Jay had begged him to stop, and the only reason he had stopped was because of me. Sandy said that she knew he was lying when he was telling the story.

But then she was more interested in what happened on our date. "Did you two do anything interesting while you were out?"

"Oh, yeah, I met Jay's Uncle Jim."

"Yeah, I'm sure that was a treat! You know I'm talking about you and Jay. Did you do it or what?" Sandy was getting upset because she was not getting the answers she wanted to hear.

"Well, we sort of ...," I teased her.

"Sort of, how could you sort of do it? Either you did it or you didn't do it. So which is it?" Sandy had worked herself up into a fit, and I couldn't stop laughing. Then I told her I'd tell her what happened after school. She said,

"Who, Sandy? I hope you are not trying to get Walter and me back together again."

"No, Girl, you need an older man, and I have just the one you need."

"Have you dated him already? It won't be the first time you've tried to pass off one of your ex's on me, for a small fee on his part. I'm telling you now, Sandy, I'm not dating or going out with whomever it is, because Jay and I are in love."

"Just wait, you'll be pleased when you see him." Walter and his flunky walked in and headed for our study section.

"Hi Louise, where's your man?" Walter asked with an attitude. "Minding his own business, like you should be doing," I snapped.

"Yeah, I saw you when I passed by the Royal Castle, letting him kiss all over you like that. You never let me kiss you like that when I had you."

"Walter, you never had me," I said.

"I did have you, until you ran out on me," Walter said, with an angry look on his face. I knew he was looking for a fight, and I didn't want any part of it. I refused to fight with Walter. I gathered my books and started to walk away. He grabbed my arm, and I fell back into the chair. Walter leaned over and asked me, "Did he have you Saturday night?" All eyes were on me, and Walter was looking crazy. I pushed him away and got back up.

"I'm not talking to you about Jay, so please get out of my face."

"So now I guess you're going to tell your man that I was bothering you huh!? Well you tell that M— F—, the next time he wants to fight, me and my boy Horace got something for him."

Walter didn't know that Jay was out of town and wouldn't be back for months. He was trying to push all of my buttons. Walter wanted my attention, even if it was negative attention, just as long as I was talking to him. I went to another section and sat down. Walter followed me there. Then he grabbed my hand and tried to kiss it. I snatched it away. "Stop fighting it," Walter said. He knew that he was pissing me off, but I wouldn't give him the fight he wanted.

"Go! Just go," I waved Walter away like he was a fly and looked in another direction.

"I'm going alright. I'm going to get you back, and you can tell your man I said so." Walter still had a thing for me, and I knew it. But it didn't matter, I loved Jay. I finished the rest of my classes for the day and met Sandy after school. She was excited to see me.

"Come on, hurry up! They're parked on the side of the school," Sandy shouted.

"Who's parked on the side of the school?"

"The guys I told you about." Sandy hurried down the sidewalk.

"OK, what is the big deal?" I asked. Sandy and I hurried down the sidewalk, almost running. We pushed past the other kids on the crowded walkway. Sandy stayed in front of me, leading the way to the car where her friends were. After we got past the crowd, and once she slowed down, she started walking flirtatiously. I knew that they must be somewhere close by.

Sandy stopped by a car that was parked on the corner and was leaning on it, talking to the driver. When I got closer to the car, I realized that her friends were and looked at me, then back into the car and smiled, "Ben, Mack, Charles, I'd like you to meet Louise."

"Hi guys, glad to meet you," I said. They all looked like a pack of wolves to me, and I didn't plan on being one of their unsuspecting little lambs. Sandy was supposed to be the smarter one between the two of us, but I'd noticed lately she could take a few tips from me. I looked at Sandy with disapproval in my eyes, but she wouldn't acknowledge my anger. Sandy got in the front seat next to Ben, the driver. She tried to wave me into the car with the two guys in the backseat. One of them smiled, got out and the other one slid over so that I could get in the middle.

I backed up away from the car. "No thanks, Guys. I'll walk home," I said and began to walk in the direction of my house. I could hear Sandy slam the door when she got out of the car. She told the driver to go on without us. He told her to call him later at work.

Once she caught up with me she blurted out, "Louise wait."

I stopped and turned around. She could see the anger in my face. "What Sandy?"

She was angry too. "What's wrong with you? They were only going to drive us around for a little while and then take us home."

"Sandy, where did you meet those guys? They are old enough to be our dad!" "So, what! They only wanted to talk, Louise."

"Well Sandy, I didn't feel safe with them," I explained.

"You just need to grow up," she said.

"And you need to slow down," I told her. We walked all the way home without talking to each other. Whenever we got mad with each other like that, we wouldn't speak to each other for weeks. After that day we didn't speak for two weeks.

The next time I saw Sandy, we were in the hall between classes at school, and everyone was crying. We had just heard the news over the PA system that Dr. Martin Luther King Jr. had been assassinated. Sandy and I cried together as we sat on the bus bench in front of the school. That was a sad day for both of us. We forgot that we were mad at each other.

When I got home Mama was crying so hard, it was as if someone had shot Daddy. Mama took to her bed for almost two days. Mama said, "They've already killed the President, and now it's Dr. King." Mama said that the world was coming to an end. I was sad about Dr.

King too, but I didn't want to hear Mama say that because I had not yet turned 16 or had a chance to do any of the things I wanted to do. And please don't let Mama say, "Mark My Words," because when Mama says that, something was going to happen.

After the sadness and gloom left our house, things started to go back to being normal.

Sandy finally came over to visit me. She had been seeing Ben, the driver, regularly. He was buying her things and giving her money to keep her interested in him, and it seemed to be working. But Ben was a married man, and Sandy knew it. Sandy also had a boyfriend that went to our school. He was on the football team. His name was Sid, but everyone called him #99. Sid loved the ground Sandy walked on, but she was no good for him. She said that Sid was a good kisser, but she needed a man with money and a car, and Sid had neither.

I had begun to see another side of Sandy, the side Mama once told me about. Mama told me that Sandy wasn't the kind of girl that I should hang around Even when I had sex with Jay, it wasn't because Sandy kept telling me that being a virgin was a bad thing, and that I should sleep with Jay. I did it because I was ready to, and I loved Jay.

While those thoughts were going through my head, Sandy turned on WAME, the radio station I loved to listen to. They were playing that song again by Betty Wright, "Tonight is the Night." We started singing along with her. Sandy liked it too. Sandy reminded me that Betty lived near our neighborhood. "Louise, did you know that Betty Wright goes to school at Allapatha Jr. High? She's always in their talent show or something."

"How do you know all of that?"

"She has a lot of brothers. I know one of them. Your sister Claire should know Betty; they should be in the same grade."

"I'll have to ask Claire."

"She was at the Island Club the other night. Ben said that Clyde Killins is promoting her."

I didn't have a clue what that meant, but I knew that Sandy was letting me know that she was a social butterfly since she'd started dating Ben. "How do you know that she was at the Island Club?"

"Ben took me there, of course."

"What did your dad say when Ben picked you up, and he saw how old Ben was?"

"I didn't let Ben come to my house. I told my dad that you and I were going to a party. Dad thought that I walked around the corner to your house. But I actually walked to the end of the corner by your house, and Ben picked me up."

"When did all of this happen?" I asked. "Last Friday."

"Sandy, you could have gotten me into trouble! Please don't do that again.

And we weren't even talking last Friday!"

"That's why I said that I was going to your house. I knew you wouldn't call the house while I was gone." Along with everything else, Sandy was turning out to be full of lies. She finally got around to ask about Jay and me because she didn't want me to start talking about how old Ben was. "Have you heard from Jay?"

"Yeah, I got a letter last week."

"I know that you miss him. What's he up to?"

"Jay got a part time job at a car plant, it's called Fleetwood. He works the second shift. He also helps his uncles run their night club."

"Well, since Jay's such a working man, I hope he's sending you some of that money."

"Jay sends me money all the time, but I can't spend it because Mom will want to know where I got the money from. And you know they don't approve of us getting money from anyone but them."

"How much did you have him send you?"

"I never ask Jay for money, he just sends it."

"Well, if the money is causing you problems, I'll take it off of your hands. My folks don't care where we get money from as long as we don't ask them for it."

"You don't have to bother taking it off of my hands; I already have plans for it when I go on my vacation."

"Where are you going?" Sandy asked with her ears all perked up.

"I don't know. I may visit my cousins in Tallahassee, or I might visit my man in Detroit," I boasted with a smile.

"Yeah, you'd better smile. Because you know that you're not even going to visit your cousin, without your mom in your face. And forget about your man in Detroit." I knew that Sandy was telling the truth, so I couldn't get mad. We looked at each other and had a good laugh. I had not gotten around to telling Sandy that Ms. Lynn had offered to pay for me to go to Detroit for the summer for my graduation present. I told Ms. Lynn that I had to ask my parents. I never got back to her with an answer, but I'd already made one up. I knew that Mama would say no, so I was going to lie and say that it was OK with my parents, but I needed a plan.

I needed to find a way to keep Mama and Ms. Lynn from talking to each other about the trip to Detroit for the summer. I had to find a way to pack my clothes and get my things from my house to Ms. Lynn's house, and be there the night that they left for Miami International Airport. I had two masters of deception on hand, Sandy and Joy, but I had to choose the right time for them to help me.

Sandy wanted to talk about Ben and how he got her a fake ID. She'd already told me that she could get fake ID's, and if I ever wanted to get into the Island Club, she'd get our ID. "What about Joy, can you get one for her?"

"Ben will have to get an ID for you first. I have one now, and Joy already has one. I saw her in The Club when Ben took me. As Sandy was talking about getting into The Club, I knew that she was just the person to help me with my plan. And I already knew that Joy was good at getting out of the house. I was the only one in the group that had not been inside a Club. Joy was Jay's little sister, and she had been out and around more than I had. At that moment I thought about her brother Gene and what he had said at the Sunday dinner I'd shared with them.

"OK, Sandy, will you ask Ben to get an ID for me? Maybe the three of us girls can go to the Island Club on Friday night."

"Girls? What about Ben?" Sandy asked with a frown.

"What about him? Do you have to ask Daddy Ben if you can go out without him?"

"No, I don't have to ask Ben anything. He didn't even get your ID yet, and already you don't want to include him."

"That's right. Ben doesn't have to go."

"Then how will we get there?" Sandy thought she had to have a man on her arm every time she went somewhere.

"We'll take a taxi." I wanted to go to The Club, but it seemed that if Ben went with us, it would have been like somebody's dad was babysitting us that night. Sandy and I saw Ben in a completely different way.

"OK, we'll pay for the taxi three ways, and everyone will buy her own drinks."

"I'll call Joy tonight," I said smiling to myself. I knew Sandy didn't like our little arrangement, but she went along with it. I needed an outfit to wear to The Club, but what do you wear to a Night Club, I wondered. I'll have to go shopping after school.

"What are you going to wear Louise? And please don't pull out any of that school stuff. Bring some of that cash from your stash that Jay sent you to school. We'll do some shopping after school."

After school the next day, Sandy and I went shopping. At first everything I wanted to buy, Sandy kept telling me that I shouldn't get it, and that I needed to get away from that school girl look. She said that I needed to look grown-up and hot. We finally ran across a cute little red and blue number. I even felt grown-up in that outfit. I loved it, but I had to let Sandy keep it at her house until that Friday night.

By the middle of the week Sandy came to my house, and as we walked down to the park, she gave me my fake ID. I was so happy, I could jump for joy. When I got back into the house, I tried to contain myself hoping that no one asked me any questions. In my house a person could get grounded for being too happy. Daddy said that we were thinking of doing something we shouldn't be doing when we got too happy.

Anyway by Friday night we had all gotten permission to go to this party we'd made up. Sandy and Joy met me at my house. I got dressed, and we went back to Sandy's house. Everything was clear because her mom was at work, and her dad was at his Friday night card game. While I was changing my clothes, Sandy changed her dress too. It was something she could never wear in front of Mama. We called a taxi and had him meet us at the corner store.

CHAPTER 11

A Night at the Island Club

O n the way to the Island Club, Sandy, Joy and I were sitting in the back of the taxi arguing about the fare. The driver finally said, "The fare is going to be three dollars, do you have it or not?" The taxi driver had pulled over to the side of the road, turned around and was looking at us. I thought he was going to put us out, but he told us to relax and that he didn't think we were old enough to go into a night club. He was looking at me as he talked. I took out a dollar, and so did Joy and Sandy. We gave it to the driver so that he would shut up. We closed our purses acting as if we had given ten dollars each, and we waved him around to the front seat.

The driver shook his head. I could see him scribbling something on his little clipboard lying next to him. Then he turned back around and told us if we called that number that he would come back to pick us up. He gave us the piece of paper that he had written on, with his name, along with a phone number.

The taxi driver's name was Harry. He looked as though he could have been a concerned friend of one of our parents trying to look out for us. I took the number from Harry and put it in my purse. Harry was pulling up in front of the Island Club. We got out and went to the door; a bouncer was standing there checking ID's. Joy and Sandy walked in, but the bouncer asked me for my ID. I turned around to see if Harry was still there, and then I looked in my purse, but the bouncer guy pushed me on through. I looked back again, and Harry was just pulling off as he waved goodbye. I kept thinking that I'd seen him somewhere before, but there was no time to think about Harry. I had to catch up with my girls.

I walked around The Club looking for them. It was crowded and smoke was everywhere. The more I looked, the angrier I got. Why didn't they wait for me? Finally through all of the smoke, I saw them sitting at a table smoking. As I pushed my way through the crowd, I got pinched on the butt twice and once on the breast. The floor was crowded, and I couldn't really see who did such a vile thing. But my focus was on getting to my table, so I kept walking until I got to our table. I sat down and thought I'd never come back to this place ever again; it had already been a bad experience. Once I got settled, I let Sandy and Joy have it for leaving me at the door and not even waiting to see if I got in or not.

"Why did you leave me at the door like that?" I demanded to know.

"You had an ID, and we didn't want it to look like it was a big deal," Joy explained.

"That's right, and you see how crowded it is tonight. We had to hurry and find a table, so stop crying because you got lost," Sandy said, as she waved the waitress to our table. We ordered three Long Island Ice Teas and two packs of Kools for Sandy and Joy. We looked around the room to see if we knew anyone. I didn't know who Sandy and Joy were looking for, but I was looking and praying that I didn't see any of Mama's friends there. So far the coast was clear. I told Sandy and Joy what had happened to me on the way to the table, and they thought it was funny. I was still a little shocked and didn't see the humor at first, but after thinking about it, I joined in and laughed too.

The D. J. was playing music before the show started. It was Talent Night at the Island Club, and everyone was there. The waitress finally brought us our drinks, and the D. J. was playing a Supremes Album. As I sipped my drink, I listened to the words Diana Ross was singing, "Love is here and oh my darling now you're gone." I was half way through my Long Island Iced Tea when I thought about Jay. I began to miss him even more, and I started to cry.

"I miss Jay so much," I cried.

"Put that drink down. You're not missing Jay, you're getting drunk," Sandy insisted, as she reached for my drink.

"How do you know? Maybe she does miss my brother," Joy argued.

"I'm OK, please don't fight. I'm going to the bathroom," I said. As I walked away from the table I could hear them saying that it was time to leave. I didn't turn around to argue because I had to pee, and I didn't know exactly where the bathroom was, so I kept walking. When I got into the bathroom, I peed, washed my hands and checked my hair and lipstick, and walked out. As I was returning to my seat, I bumped into Ben. I tried to get his attention so I could show him where Sandy was. I knew if Ben was sitting at our table, she'd forget about leaving. I started to grab Ben's arm, but I noticed that a lady was holding his hand. I knew right away that she was Ben's wife. I hurried past both of them, so that I could prepare Sandy for what was coming.

When I got to the table I sat down and looked at Sandy. My eyes must have said that something was wrong, but I couldn't say anything at first.

"What the hell is wrong with you now?"

"Sandy, don't look now, but Ben is coming this way," I blurted out.

"Where? I can't wait to see My Baby," she said with a smile. But when Sandy turned around, Ben was coming toward us with his wife. Sandy quickly turned back around to finish her drink, and the look on her face broke my heart. When she looked up at me, her eyes were raining tears. Joy looked at Sandy and then at me; she didn't know what was going on. She didn't know Ben and that he was a married man. Ben and his wife got a table right in back of ours. They sat down and Ben waved the waitress to their table. I told Joy that the guy was Ben, a friend of Sandy's.

"If that's Ben, who's the b—?" Joy was still confused. I explained to Joy that Ben was a married man, and that was his wife. "Well Sandy, what the hell are you crying for? You know what's up." Joy finished her drink, and we all got up from the table and left.

As we walked out, Sandy and Ben's eyes met. I saw Ben's wife watching him look at Sandy, and I pushed her along to get her out of there. When we got to the front entrance, I saw a pay phone. I got the number that Harry, the taxi driver, had given us and called it.

Joy and Sandy looked a little tipsy to me. I'd noticed when we were inside at the table, Sandy had one, tall, empty glass in front of her, and she'd finished another. Joy had two, empty glasses in front of her. I never got to finish my first drink. Sandy kept looking back at the door like she wanted to go back inside. "I have half a mind to go back in there and tell Ben off," she said.

"Tell Ben off, for what, Sandy?" I asked.

"Tell him off for bringing her here; Ben said that this was our spot."

"Well the half a mind that wants to go back inside is drunk, so let's go." Sandy blamed me for what had happened, because I didn't want Ben to go to The Club with us that night. She said that's why he took his wife there. "Sandy, did you really believe Ben when he said this spot was for you and him?" I asked.

"Of course not, but I'm coming back, and I'll show him." Sandy had decided that they would go back to the Island Club after they dropped me off at home. I saw a Liberty Cab drive up to the door; it was Harry. We all got into the cab. Once we settled our fare, I reminded them that we all had to go to my front door together, and I also had to change clothes. Sandy said that we should go to her house. I could change my clothes there because her dad didn't get home from his card parties until the next day.

When Harry drove us up to the corner store, they told Harry to wait for them or come back there in thirty minuets. He looked at us with disappointed eyes. He shook his head, but he agreed to come back for them. As we all walked back to my house, I said, "Did you see how Harry looked at us, he must think we're little liars."

"Fu— Harry, and we are! Little liars, but who cares what Harry thinks?" Sandy blurted out, as we walked as fast as we could. We all laughed. Sandy and Joy took turns talking about Harry.

"That's right, you see that bit— took our money, and he's coming back to get some more," Joy added. We all laughed so hard we had to stop for awhile to get ourselves together. Joy always used the B word. She called everyone a b— if they made her mad, male or female. We went to Sandy's house as planned. I changed my clothes, and as we walked through her living room, I grabbed about five pieces of Juicy Fruit gum from her mom's lazy-susan dish on the coffee table. I put all five pieces in my mouth, so Daddy wouldn't smell alcohol on my breath. Sandy sprayed my hair with some of her Afro Sheen, and since I'd already changed my clothes, I didn't smell like smoke either.

It was ten-thirty when I got home. I knocked on the door, and Daddy opened it. He was glad that I had gotten home early. He didn't even ask me a dozen questions before I was allowed to go to bed. He said goodnight to Joy and Sandy and closed the door.

The next day was Saturday. When I got up that morning, I couldn't help but wonder what had happened to Joy and Sandy after they dropped me off that night. Then I thought about my dress that I'd worn to The Club. I'd stuffed it into my shoulder bag before I left Sandy's house that night. I got up and opened my bag. As I was taking the dress out of the bag, Bobbie walked in. I was trying to put it in the back of the closet. I thought she'd just keep on doing whatever she'd come in the room to do, but she stood there and asked, "Oh! Louise let me see that dress; it's so cute. Whose is it?"

I had to tell her the truth. If we were going to be friends and sisters like we were before, this would be our test, and we would sink or swim. "It belongs to me. I wore it to the Island Club last night."

"The Island Club, you mean you went inside?"

"Of course, I went inside. Last night was talent night," I told her. If she only knew the whole story, but all she had to know was that I had been in a night club, and that I'd changed clothes after I'd left the house. We were supposed to be close again, and I didn't want to have to hide that night at The Club from her too. It was going to be stressful enough trying to keep it from Daddy.

"And you had on that dress?" she asked. Bobbie put the dress up in front of herself and looked in the mirror, and then she looked at me.

"Yeah, you can borrow it anytime you like." She smiled and gave me a big hug. After we started to talk, I learned that Rico had taken her out of town to a party the week before. I also had some news to share. "Bobbie, please don't tell, but Jay has been sending me money, but I've been too afraid to spend it because Mama would want to know where the money came from."

Bobbie got up and looked outside of our bedroom door to see if anyone was listening. Then she hurried back to the bed, and she confessed, "Louise the same thing is going on with me. Rico gives me money all the time, but I can't spend it for the same reasons. It felt good that Bobbie and I were sharing secrets again. We talked and giggled about everything. An hour passed before we knew it.

Then Mama called Bobbie, and I realized that I had not opened the letter that I had gotten from Jay. When I opened the envelope, five, ten-dollar bills fell out of it. In the letter Jay said that it was just a little something special for Easter to let me know that he was thinking of me. Then he wrote how much he loved and missed me. He wrote how many times he'd had flashbacks of our last night together.

But at the end of the letter he wrote,

Louise,

I have some sad news for if you haven't already heard it through the media.

Li'l Bobby Hutton, of the Black Panther Party, was killed by the police, and so was Eldridge Cleaver. They said that when Eldridge came out of the house, he had been brutally beaten by "The Pigs." And Li'l Bobby already had his hands in the air when they fired on him.

I knew that you'd want to know all of the details. We always had long conversations about the Panthers, and I know you care about them. I'm sorry I'm not there to comfort you.

Love Ya, JAY

I cried for Lil Bobby, and I cried for Eldridge too. I didn't know them personally, but they were Black Panther members, and just knowing about their purpose made me feel like I was somebody, when white America was telling me that I wasn't. I was still crying when Bobbie and Mama passed by the door. I still had Jay's letter in my hand, and they thought something had happened to Jay. Mama rushed in and sat on the bed next to me. She asked me what had happened, but when I told her about Lil Bobby and Eldridge, she stood up and said, "Girl, you don't even know them boys. What you crying for?"

I dried my eyes and put away my letter. I knew that Mama didn't understand me or the Black Panther Party. She and Daddy had accepted segregation, and in their minds, "That's just the way things were."

"Come on Mama. Let's just let her be by herself. She's upset now," Bobbie said. She was never into the Panthers, but she knew that they were very important to me and that I tried to keep up with their movement. I was thankful that she was trying to get Mama off of me.

Mama walked out of the room with Bobbie. Then she turned and said as she pointed her finger at me, with an angry look on her face, "You even got your sister Claire dressing and talking like them Black Panther fools. I hope she doesn't loose her mind too." Although when I think back, Claire was becoming a little Angela Davis. She was also pro–Panther Party, but in our house she had to keep a low profile. In our house, if your ideas were different from Daddy's, you had to put up walls around your mind because Daddy would wear you down, until you thought the way he did.

After Mama left my room, I lay across the bed and went to sleep. When I got up later that day, Joy called me. She said that Ms. Lynn had invited me to dinner. I said I'd come, but I had to ask my parents first. I asked Joy what had happened to her and Sandy that night. "Sandy went back to The Club, and I went to stay with some friends, and we had a party over there." Joy answered.

"What did Ms. Lynn say when you got in?" I asked.

"Ms. Lynn didn't say anything. She had to work overtime, and she got in around noon herself."

"What about your dad?"

"He stays at his girlfriend's house on Friday nights." "Does your mom know about her?"

"Yeah! But she is in denial."

Sandy had gone back to the Island Club to confront Ben. I had to call her. I told Joy thanks for the invitation, and that I'd call her later. I hung up and called Sandy right away. The phone rang and rang, and then finally someone picked up. "Hello, Sandy, is that you?" I asked. I could hear her dad arguing in the background. He was telling Sandy that she was a slut, and that young ladies didn't do what she'd done that night. I thought to myself, Sandy must have gotten in mighty late after she left The Club. Her father had beaten her home from his card game. I tried to get off the phone as soon as I could. It's awful when your parents are fussing at you, and you're on the phone.

"OK, Sandy. I'll call you later."

"Yeah, I guess you can hear. I got in really late last night. Call me," she said very softly; then she hung up. It sounded like Sandy had really gotten herself into some deep trouble this time. She was my friend, and I had to help her if I could. I didn't know how, but I had to try. The first thing I needed to do was find out what had happened. Sandy's father had to pick her mother up from work; she was a nurse at North Miami General Hospital. It was about an hour away from Sandy's house. When he left to go and pick her up, Sandy called me back. The phone rang, and I rushed to pick it up.

"Hello."

"Hi Louise, this is Sandy."

"Hey Girl, what happened last night?"

"Well, when I got back to The Club, Ben was still there with his wife." "Did he see you?"

"Yeah! But I acted like I didn't see him. I started flirting with every man that I saw at the bar to get Ben's attention, and the next thing I knew, Ben and his wife were leaving. As they passed the bar, I flirted with the bouncer. He was on a break, and he had let me in when I went back after dropping you off. Even though I had an ID, he said that he knew I wasn't old enough to get in. But he liked me, and I could get in anytime he was on the door.

When I looked in the mirror behind the bar, I could see Ben had returned and was standing in back of me. The bouncer saw him too. He told me he had to go, and he left me there with Ben. Ben took me by the arm and led me to the table where he and his wife had been sitting. When I sat down, Ben told me that he didn't like the way I'd been flirting at the bar. The waitress came over to our table, and Ben ordered me another drink. I told him I'd had enough to drink.

I got up from the table because the frown on Ben's face scared me. I'd never seen that side of Ben before. He pulled me back down by my arm; I almost fell out of the chair. I was in tears. Then he went on and on about how he's not one of my little school mates and not to play with him, because he's not a toy. He gave me his handkerchief and told me to dry my eyes so that we could leave. Then he took me by the arm, and I grabbed my purse, and we left."

"Where did you go?" I asked her.

"We sat in his car for about half an hour. He lectured me like I was his kid. Then he wanted to kiss and make out. I was so mad at him, I said, "No, take me home.""

Then he said, "Let's go to a motel."

I said, "No." He pulled me down on the front seat; he tore off my underwear and forced himself on me. After it was over, he told me that I should never refuse him again. He tried to kiss me again. I didn't want to, but I was too scared not to. He held me until I stopped crying, telling me that he was sorry and that he loved me.

After I stopped crying, Ben drove me home. I opened the door to get out, and he took my purse from me and put a one-hundred dollar bill in it and told me to call him at work tonight.

"Didn't you try to push him off of you or scream or something?" I was so upset with Ben I could hardly believe how calm Sandy was.

"Of course, I tried to push him off of me, but I didn't scream. I didn't want to get him in trouble, and I sure didn't want the police taking me home," she explained.

"What happened when you got home?"

"I went to the door, and my old man slapped me and snatched me into the house. And after he cussed me out, he told me to go to bed."

"You mean you didn't tell your dad what happened?"

"No! Because he would have said it serves you right for getting in the car with him. Look, I was in the wrong place at the wrong time anyway. I just have to forget about it. I'm just not going to see Ben anymore.

Ben had raped my friend, and she said there was nothing that she could do about it. I had a rude awakening that day. I couldn't understand how someone could say that they loved you, and then turn around and hurt you like that.

CHAPTER 12

The Plan

M s. Lynn had invited me to dinner. I knew that she wanted to know if I had permission to accept her graduation gift, a round-trip ticket to Detroit for the summer. All Mama had to do was say, yes, but I knew that wasn't going to happen. Mama would make me stay home for a month of Sundays or even ground me for life just for asking.

When I got to her house, she greeted me as soon as I got inside. Smiling as if she knew I had good news for her, the first thing she said was, "Louise! What did your mom say about the trip?" Still smiling, she waited for an answer. I didn't want to lie, but I had to. I couldn't let them leave without me.

So smiling just as hard as Ms. Lynn, I said, "Yes, Mama said, 'Yes,' I can go too." When I heard myself say, "Yes," I realized that I was becoming just as bad as Sandy and Joy, the "masters of deception." After all of Daddy's Rules, I had become just as bad as the same kind of people he'd always put down. I hoped that Ms. Lynn didn't really want to go into details and want to call Mama and discuss travel plans, like I knew Mama would have done. But strangely enough she didn't. We had another good and tasty meal with good conversation.

When we finished eating, Joy and I went into the living room. I sat on the couch, and Joy sat right next to me and whispered, "Girl, that was some hot lie you told my mom in there."

"I know Joy; you've got to help me." We went into her room that she shared with her sister Sue. We both agreed that we needed a plan. The phone rang, and it was for Joy. She went out to the living room to answer it. After she had been on the phone for a while, Sue and I started to talk about the trip.

Sue told me that their mother had some issues. She said that sometimes Ms. Lynn did things or made decisions that were not rational and not even realize it. "Louise, I know she seems like a very nice person, and she is. But just think, who do you know that would do what Mom is doing for their son's girlfriend? Mom doesn't really know you; she has only met you twice. And now she wants to give you an all-expense, paid trip to Detroit where your boyfriend, her son, is staying, without calling your mother? And Louise, don't get me wrong, I like you, and I hope you get your wish, but I just thought I'd warn you about Mom.

Sue was right about some of the things she was telling me about Ms. Lynn, and I knew it. But I didn't want to believe her because I wanted to go—no matter how I got there. I wanted to be with Jay. Sue also told me that she didn't even want to go herself, and that they were not allowed to tell their dad that they were going to Detroit that summer. That's why Ms. Lynn had to make sure that her husband went to visit his sisters that Sunday when we had dinner. She said that she didn't think that her mother intended to return to Florida. Joy had given me some hints about her mom early on, but I didn't think anything of it.

A week had passed and there was no call from Ms. Lynn to Mama. I started thinking that Sue must be right, and that was cool with me.

I could go ahead with my plan. Sandy and Joy were going to help me. I had to figure out a way to leave home. I knew that it would be a decision that would not only affect the rest of my life, but it would affect others as well. It was one of the worst decisions I'd ever made. But it was my decision to leave Miami to be with Jay in Detroit. I had not considered the effect my leaving home would have on Mama. But I was in love with Jay, and that's all that mattered at the time.

The next week Joy, Sandy and I got together to make a plan for my get-away. We all agreed that since Jay was sending me money, I could use it to buy my clothes for the trip. The first week I bought a large suitcase. Sandy let me keep it at her house, because that's where we were going to stash everything. Next we went shopping for my personals and then clothes for the summer. Across the street from the school there were department stores. There were The Three Sisters, Mc Cory's and the five and dime store. It was perfect. We'd go shopping after school, and on the way home, we'd take everything I'd bought and pack my suitcase carefully making sure that I had everything I'd need for the summer. Sometimes I could just see myself getting on that plane. But the sad part about it was that I could also see Mama crying when she realized that I was gone.

The next Friday would be the night of our Senior Prom. Mama told Daddy to give me the money for my prom dress early. That way I could get a head start on the other prom-day shoppers, and I could get the dress that I really wanted. They were wonderful about everything; it made me angry with myself for what I was doing behind their backs. I was so confused; I wanted to call the whole trip off. But I also wanted to go to Detroit to be with Jay. It was a hard decision to make. Just for the sake of an argument, I told Mama that I wanted to go to the prom stag. I knew that she'd say, "You shouldn't go to the prom stag, it does not look nice for a young lady to go to the prom unescorted." Since I was looking for a reason to get mad at her, that would do it. I'd tell them if I couldn't go to the Prom stag, I didn't want to go. Then I'd have a reason to go around and pout.

But Mama wouldn't even let me stay mad at her. She came into my room later, and she said that she and Daddy had talked it over, and it was OK for me to go to the prom stag. When Mama left my room, I closed the door and cried. I needed to have some peace about what I was going to do, but Mama wouldn't let me. As I sat on the bed thinking about what to do, Sandy called me. She wanted to know when I was going shopping for the prom, and who I was going to the prom with. I told Sandy that I was going to the party stag, and that I was going to get the #21 bus downtown at noon that day.

She wanted me to go to the prom with Sid's friend. I told her, "No." Jay wasn't there, and I didn't want to go out with any other guys. But Sandy said either I would go to the prom with Sid's friend, or she would hold my suitcase hostage. Or it just might find its way back to my house. I promptly agreed to go to the prom with Sid's friend and to meet her at the bus stop at noon. Mama got her wish after all: I had a date for the prom, but for all the wrong reasons.

CHAPTER 13

Ben Stalks Sandy

Sandy and I got a late start, which meant it would be dark by the time we got back home. Two girls on the # 21 bus going through Overtown alone was trouble—anything could happen. The last bus finally came, and we got on. I went to the two seats almost at the back of the bus and sat by the window. When I looked out of the window again, I saw Ben's car on the corner behind the bus. I told Sandy to look out of the window. When she did, she saw Ben following the bus too.

On the bus ride downtown, I could see that Sandy was very nervous. But there was always a police car across from the bus stop where we got off, so we didn't have to worry about Ben doing anything to us. "Sandy, you should run to the police when we get off the bus."

"No! I'm not going to the police on Ben; he'd never hurt me."
"What do you mean, he'd never hurt you? Ben raped you."

"Louise it's not rape if the guy is your boyfriend, and I've already told Ben that I didn't want to see him anymore." Ben didn't seem to be the type that took rejection too kindly.

When we got off of the bus, Ben pulled up beside us, and he told Sandy that he wanted to talk to her. We kept walking, and Sandy never looked in Ben's direction. But he drove a few stores down and parked the car. We hurried inside one of the stores. It had a shoe store downstairs, and all of the prom gowns were upstairs. Sandy went all the way to the back, downstairs, in the shoe store, and I ran upstairs.

No one else came into the store for awhile, so we started to look around for our prom dresses and accessories. Sandy needed yellow shoes and a yellow gown. I needed a white gown and pink shoes and a purse. I heard the door open. I could see that it was Ben. Sandy had already found her shoes, purse, stockings and something for her hair. I stayed upstairs and watched Ben. I didn't know what he might do. Just as Sandy was about to pay the store clerk, Ben pushed Sandy's money to the side and paid for all of her purchases. Sandy just smiled, took her bags, not even acknowledging that Ben was there, and went upstairs where I was to see if I was ready to get my shoes.

She had to get her gown from upstairs. Ben was right behind her. I went back downstairs, bought my shoes and purse, and was headed out of the door, when I heard Sandy and Ben arguing. I knew then from the conversation they were having that they'd be back together soon. It was dark by that time, so Ben drove us home. They dropped me off on the corner by my house and went their own way.

Sid's friend called me the next day. We got acquainted and agreed on what time he'd pick me up on prom night. At first I was mad with him because of the way we were thrown together. But Milton, my prom date, was a nice guy, and he had no idea of how we'd gotten hooked up. I didn't see Sandy until the night of the prom. We didn't even go shopping that week after school; she was avoiding me because she didn't want to hear what I had to say about Ben. Sandy had Sid meet her at the front door of the hotel where we had the prom.

CHAPTER 14

Prom Night

While we were waiting for Sandy to come, Milton, Sid, and I walked around in the lobby talking to our other classmates. I excused myself for a moment to go to the restroom, and on the way there, I looked outside the lobby's doors, and I saw Sandy getting out of Ben's car. How could she, I thought? How could she use Sid like that? She'd used Milton and me too—just so that she and Ben could be together. I waited until she got inside of the hotel; I had something to tell her.

When Sandy walked into the lobby, she was glad to see me. She hurried across the room where I was. "Louise! Where are Sid and Milton?" she asked, as her eyes glanced around the lobby, wondering if Sid had watched her get out of Ben's car.

"They are inside checking the cost of the pictures. And Sandy, you can stop looking now. Sid didn't see you get out of the car with Ben, but I did."

"What's wrong with you?" she asked, as if she'd done nothing wrong. "Sandy, you used all of us just so you could get to be with Ben."

"Oh, mind your own business and find your date, because I'm going to find mine."

"Find what date, you mean the one that you hooked up? Maybe everyone should know what's really going on!"

'I'll tell you what's going on, Heifer. Don't forget that your little suitcase is at my house, and I could just let your little secret slip out."

"OK, you do that, Heifer, and I'm going to just let it slip out that Ben raped you. I wonder what your dad would do to that dirty, old, married man!"

We heard Sid and Milton coming into the lobby. They were asking each other where we were. Sandy and I walked over and met them at the door. Sid could see that we were both upset. He asked Sandy, "What's wrong Honey? Did someone out here say something to you?"

Sandy looked at me and rolled her eyes. Then she took Sid by the hand and walked over to the area where they were taking pictures. Milton asked me what was wrong; he'd realized that Sandy and I had been arguing.

I told Milton that everything was OK and that I'd like a cold drink. He walked me over to a table that seated four. I sat down while Milton went to get me some punch. I could see Milton waving for Sandy and Sid to go over to the table where I was sitting. Sid walked Sandy to the table and went to the punch bowl to join Milton in bringing our drinks. While they got our punch, we finished our little discussion. Sandy reminded me of all the things she knew about me, and I said that I had a list of things that I could tell on her. We soon realized that we sounded like a couple of ten year-olds and started laughing.

Sid and Milton came back to the table and found that we'd made up. They looked at each other and gave a sigh of relief. We sat around and laughed and talked for awhile. Our class leaders said their speeches, and the rest of the evening went well. At the end of the night the D.J. played music that made me wish Jay was there. And Milton tried his best to make me forget him. I'd told Milton all night that I didn't want to dance with him on slow records. On the last dance for that night the D.J. played Smokey Robinson and The Miracles, "Oh-oh-oh Baby," and Milton refused to hear, "No" for an answer, so I danced with him.

I was OK after the dance. My feelings never changed about Jay because I knew that I loved him. But Milton told me that he'd fallen for me, and he wanted to see me again. I told him that there was no chance of us getting together. He even wanted me to let him take me out just to have some fun, and when Jay got back, he'd step aside. I still said, "No." Milton called me a couple of times after that night to let me know when our prom pictures were coming back. He dropped them off one night when they came, and we agreed not to see each other again.

CHAPTER 15

Leaving Miami

Weeks had gone by, and I had everything I needed for my vacation. Jay was sending me money every week, and I was saving it. Since I'd made up my mind to go to Detroit, I thought about Jay all the time. And I told myself that Mama wouldn't miss me; she'd have Bobbie. She was such a well-rounded child. They'd be glad that I was gone. I was looking for reasons why it was OK for me to leave because deep inside I felt bad about what I was about to do. I also told myself that I'd go to Detroit for the summer, and then I'd come back and face the music, even if I was grounded for life. But I knew in my heart that once I left Miami, my whole life would change, and that I wouldn't be right back.

The next week I graduated from Jackson Sr. High School. That night was a fog. I just went through the motions. My mind was on getting to Detroit to be with Jay.

The second part of the plan was to get me and my suitcase to Ms. Lynn's house. On the usual Friday, Sandy's father took her mother to work, and then he'd go to his poker game. When they left, Sandy called Ben to come over and take her and my suitcase to Ms. Lynn's house. I told

Mama that I was going to walk around to Sandy's house, but I went to the corner store and called Harry, the cab driver. Harry came right away. I gave him the address, and he took me to Opa-Locka, where I found Ben and Sandy, Joy and her sister waiting for me in front of the house.

Sandy asked me if I remembered to leave Bobbie the note and what did I write on it? I said, "Yes," I did write the note for Bobbie. I left it on her bed. I wrote:

Bobbie, By the time you find this note, I'll be gone already. I'm alright and nothing has happened to me. This is something I have to do. I love you all, and I'll contact you later. Love Ya, Louise Joy invited everyone to come inside; we sat around on their front porch listening to music and having some snacks. Ms. Lynn came out on the porch with us. She said, "Good evening," to everyone and asked if Ben was someone's dad or uncle. Sandy said, No, that Ben was a friend of hers, and her attitude let Ms. Lynn know that Ben was someone that Sandy was dating. After that, Ben and Sandy walked to the door. I gave her a big hug, and we said goodbye.

Everyone had their bags packed, and Ms. Lynn went to the phone and called a cab. In twenty minutes, I found myself getting into a cab and heading for the airport. On the way there, Joy asked me if I was alright. I said that I was OK, but I was thinking about things I should have thought about earlier; but they hadn't seemed important then. It was only at the eleventh hour, that I wondered why Ms. Lynn hadn't called Mama before we left, to let her know at least when we'd be back. And it was only at the last minute that I realized that I should have called Jay to let him know what my plans were. But I kept telling myself that everything was going to be alright, and not to stress.

After we got to the airport, I forgot all about how sad I'd been. I was on a mission. I had to see Jay. I said to myself, from this point on, it's going to be all new experiences for me. My first trip out of town without Mama looking over my shoulder. My first plane ride. And I could do what ever I wanted to do!

CHAPTER 16

Baltimore

After we got to the airport, we checked our bags and boarded the plane. I was so excited; I was looking around checking everything out. We were flying coach, but I didn't know the difference. We were on an airplane, and that was all First Class to me. Joy and I sat together, and Sue and Ms. Lynn sat together. They gave us a light snack and a beverage to drink. After a couple of hours in the air, we all went to sleep. When I woke up again, Ms. Lynn was telling us it was time to get off of the plane. I wanted to see what Detroit looked like flying into the city at night, but I'd missed it. We gathered our sweaters and purses and got off.

Ms. Lynn said that we had to go to baggage claim. We picked up our bags, and we went outside where Ms. Lynn said that we had to catch a cab. Joy asked her why Jay and Uncle Lenny weren't there to pick us up. I thought that maybe they were at The Club or something. Ms. Lynn waved down a cab and told us to get in. She never answered Joy's question, so Joy asked her again when we got into the cab. She told Joy to stop asking so many questions. The driver put our luggage into the trunk, got in, and asked Ms. Lynn where she was headed. She gave the driver a card. He said it would take about an hour to get to that address, and the fare would be fifteen dollars. Ms. Lynn said, OK. The driver asked us, "Have you girls ever been to Baltimore before?"

"No, that's why we flew into Detroit," Joy answered with an attitude, thinking that she was in Detroit.

The driver laughed and looked back at her. "You have a strange since of humor, or is that my clue to mind my own business?" I began to feel sick; I had a burning feeling in the pit of my stomach. I knew that something was wrong.

Ms. Lynn still had not said anything.

I asked the driver, with my eyes closed, "What part of Detroit are we in anyway?"

The driver turned around and looked at us for a minute and asked, "What's wrong with you people? You are in Baltimore! OK? Welcome to Baltimore."

Ms. Lynn said that she didn't want to hear a word out of anyone. I'd never seen that side of Ms. Lynn before. I looked at Sue and remembered what she'd told me in her room about Ms. Lynn. I just closed my eyes and kept them closed for the rest of the ride.

After riding for about an hour, the driver drove up to a four-story building that needed lots of repairs. The cement walkway was about half a block long. It had cracks and large pieces missing out of it, and weeds growing up each side of it. The driver took our luggage out of the trunk and put it on the edge of the walkway, but only after Ms. Lynn paid our fare. We had to drag our own luggage to the front door.

I started to cry inside; I knew that I'd made a wrong decision, but it was too late then. It was a long way home, I thought, and too late to turn back now. There were no street lights, and we could hardly see in front of us, but we managed to make our way to the front door. We must have knocked for about twenty minutes, but no one answered. Ms. Lynn said that the lady must be upstairs sleeping.

Joy, Sue, and I started to bang on the door at the same time and really loud, so that she could hear us. Finally we heard footsteps coming toward us, and then someone opened the door. But there was no light inside at first. Then someone said in a loud voice, "Hurry up and come on in!" Suddenly a light came on in the small hallway, and we rushed inside the door.

A big lady closed the door behind us. She was huge; and she had no teeth, no hair, and no manners. The big woman led us down a long hallway that smelled like pee. When we got to the end of the hall, she pointed to a large room that had three, small, twin-size beds in it. She waved us inside the room and ordered, "This is where you will sleep."

I looked in and said, "But there are only three beds in there, and there are four of us."

"Then you can sleep in the room with Dora, Miss Missy." I thought, why did I have to open my big mouth? And what is her problem? I took my suitcase into the room with Dora. When I turned the light on, I could see Miss Dora's teeth floating around in a glass on her night table. I had never seen anything like that before in my life, and I got sick again.

Miss Dora pulled the covers from her head, looked at me, smiled and said, "Hey Baby, who you are?"

She had two K-9's or fangs hanging out of her mouth that gave me a pain in the side of my neck. I put my hand around my throat and smiled at Miss Dora. She looked like a vampire. "Hi, Miss Dora," I answered. I went to sleep with a towel wrapped around my neck that night, just in case Miss Dora got any ideas. The big lady's name was Beulah. She came back to the room to let me know that she was going to put another twin bed in the large room the next morning.

I got up early the next morning. I'd watched Miss Dora all night just in case she got thirsty during the night. By daybreak I was dressed and exploring the floor that we slept on. It didn't take long for me to figure out where we were. As I walked down the hall that morning, I saw things that I hadn't noticed the night before. All of the doors to the rooms were open, and everyone in them was either blind, crippled or crazy. Ms. Lynn had taken us out of Florida and brought us to a nursing home in Baltimore.

But why did she tell me that she wanted to give me a trip to Detroit as a graduation gift when all the time, she had this in mind? But Sue had told me that her mother had issues, and I wished I had listened to her. My blood ran cold when I realized that I would never see my family again. When I managed to get my thoughts together, I heard Ms. Beulah calling out, "Hey You, get your sorry ass down here and help me push your bed into your room."

"Who me?" I asked, as I was just about to pee in my pants. My poor feelings were crushed; no one had ever talked to me like that before. The big lady had shouted so loud, everyone woke up. Joy and Sue ran out of their room into the smelly hallway to see what was going on, and Ms. Lynn was right behind them.

As we pushed the squeaky bed down the hall, toward the room where it was needed, Big Beulah looked at everyone standing in the doorway and told them, "Move out of the way. Get dressed and go downstairs to the kitchen. If you are going to work for me, you got to get up earlier than this," Beulah ordered.

Joy and Sue looked at Ms. Lynn and they asked, "Bee! What did Big Beulah mean when she said, 'Work for her?'"

"I was going to explain that to you girls, this morning at breakfast."

After we got my bed into the room, I went to Miss Dora's room and got my suitcase and said, "Good morning," to Miss Dora.

She smiled and said, "Good morning, Baby." I looked at her fangs and hurried to the other room.

As we walked down the long smelly hallway, Big Beulah walked behind us. She was six-feet, and about four-hundred pounds. She wore a black, curly wig, and when she talked, her voice was so loud it echoed throughout the house. She told us to go the dining room and to wait for her there. Joy, Sue, and I went into the dining room and sat down, expecting to be served breakfast. Beulah and Ms. Lynn went into another room to talk. We could hear them arguing about Ms. Lynn's pay and about how long we should stay there. Ms. Beulah said that if we didn't work, she would charge Ms. Lynn for our room and board. Ms. Lynn had promised Beulah that she would help her for a month until her assistant got back. Joy, Sue, and I sat at one of six, dining tables in a large dining hall, waiting for breakfast, still in a daze by Beulah's remarks.

"What has Mom done now?" Joy asked Sue, with tears streaming down her face, shaking her head in disgust. Sue just shrugged her shoulders looking at me and then at Joy. Sue tried to make light of the situation because Joy was getting upset.

"Bee may have told Big Beulah that she was going to bring a crew from Florida to help out." Sue started to laugh, and so did I, but Joy didn't see the humor. We looked around for the cook to make our breakfast, but no one came in to even put on a pot of coffee. We could hear every step Beulah took on the dull, wood floors as she walked toward us. When we couldn't hear the loud foot steps anymore, we looked at the doorway, and there stood big Beulah, even angrier than before.

In a loud and demanding voice, she shouted at us, "Get up and get those tables set for breakfast. What are you sitting there for?"

"But we haven't had any breakfast yet," Joy reminded Beulah.

"If you sat there all of this time and didn't eat breakfast, then you won't eat any. Now get started with these tables." Beulah was banging on the tables and looking at us as though she was going to beat us. She scared us so bad, we were running into each other. We knew nothing about setting up a dining room and serving people.

Then Ms. Lynn came in crying. She told us how she had gotten into a jam, and the bottom line was that we were stuck there for a month. Ms. Lynn told us what we were expected to do, and she showed each of us how to do our individual jobs. We had to set the table each morning, pour the orange juice, wash the dishes, clean the kitchen after meals, chop vegetables for the next meal, wash and hang the clothes on the clothesline, and scrub the floors. By the end of the day we were so tired that we forgot to talk about how mad we were with Beulah and Ms. Lynn.

We looked everywhere for the phone every chance we got; Ms. Beulah had hidden it. We felt like captive prisoners, and we had no contact with the outside world. Joy and Sue had found the number to their Uncle Lenny's phone. They said that they were going to call and tell Jay to come and get us. As for me, I felt that I deserved the punishment for leaving my family the way I did.

Two weeks passed, and I felt there was no hope of us ever getting out of there, and I didn't care. Each day I just went through the motions. I stopped talking to anyone. I didn't want to eat; life had no meaning. Ms. Lynn was concerned about my behavior. She said that she had to do something and soon.

One night after we'd finished all of our work, Joy went into Ms. Beulah's room, and she found the phone in Ms. Beulah's closet. She came into our room to tell everyone what she'd found. I was in the bathroom, but I could still hear her tell Sue that they were going to call Jay the next day. When Ms. Lynn came into the room, they told her too. Everyone was happy about it. Ms. Lynn agreed it was time for us to leave, and we'd call Jay and Lenny the next day. By the time everyone got showered and changed for bed, Beulah stood in the doorway and told Ms. Lynn, in her usual demanding and nasty voice, that when we got up the next morning, she wouldn't be there. She had to go to the Western Union because she'd gotten a telegram from her assistant. She was going downtown to pick it up, so we should carry on without her.

When Beulah left, Ms. Lynn told us to get some sleep, so that we could get up early the next morning and get the residents set up for breakfast. That way we all could go into Ms. Beulah's room together to call Jay while Beulah was gone. Ms. Lynn said that maybe if I talked to Jay, I'd come out of my depression.

The next day when we got up, Ms. Beulah had already gone to the Western Union. We got everything setup in the dining room and went into Ms. Beulah's room to call Jay. Ms. Lynn talked to Jim for awhile and then to Lenny. Then I heard Ms. Lynn say, "Stop it Jay," I could tell by the look in Ms. Lynn's eyes and in her voice that Jay was saying something unpleasant. Then Ms. Lynn threw the phone on the floor and told Joy to talk to her brother, but Sue picked the phone up to see why her mother was so upset. Meanwhile Joy was telling me that when she got the phone, she was going to tell her brother everything. Ms. Lynn heard Joy and went back to the dining room.

When Joy talked to Jay, she told him that their mother was a nut, and that she had told us that she was taking us to Detroit, but she'd lied and taken us to Baltimore. Joy was crying and getting angry and hysterical. Then I got upset and started to cry. Joy managed to calm herself down, and then she gave the phone to me. I took the phone from Joy and put it to my ear. At first I was too emotional to talk, but I could still hear Jay telling me to take it easy.

"J-a-a-a-y," I cried, not able to say anything else. "Hey Babe, you alright?"

"Yeah, Jay. I'm a little upset, but I'm OK."

"Babe, I'm sorry for what my mom did to all of you, and I guess I don't have to tell you by now that Ms. Lynn has some problems. We laughed about it. Then Jay told me how my parents had called his stepfather to see if he knew where I was. His stepfather told Daddy that his girls were missing too. He gave Daddy the phone number to Lenny's house. When Jay talked to Daddy, he told Daddy that he didn't know where I was and that I wasn't with him. Daddy believed Jay because they were still receiving letters for me from Jay. He told me not to worry, that they were coming to get us. Then Jay said that he wanted to speak to Ms. Lynn again. Joy called Ms. Lynn back to the phone. Jay and Ms. Lynn talked it over, and they agreed that Ms. Lynn would take us to Detroit as soon as she got paid. They hung up, and we all got out of Beulah's room.

When Ms. Beulah came back home, she told Ms. Lynn that her assistant was going to be there the next day, and she was giving Ms. Lynn her pay, but we had twenty-four hours before we were to leave. When Ms. Lynn opened her envelope, she'd only gotten half of her pay. Ms. Lynn didn't argue with Beulah because she still had enough money to get all of our plane tickets and still have a little money left over. But Ms. Lynn was still upset with Beulah; she told Beulah that we would be leaving early the next morning.

Later that night, Ms. Lynn told us to pack our clothes and be ready to leave at 6 am. Then later that night while Ms. Lynn made her rounds to see if the residents were either wet or needed changing, she gave all of them a heavy dose of laxative on her second round. She'd already called the cab in advance. She told them to have a driver at that address no later than 6:30 am. At 5:00 am, we were getting dressed, and by the smell of the fumes floating down the halls, we could tell that everyone had good results from the laxative.

By 6 am we were walking out the front door. We could hear Big Beulah walking up and down the halls cursing. She said that we had to get the residents cleaned up, but by the time she got to our room, she realized that we had packed our things, and we were out of there. She hurried to the front door; she told Ms. Lynn that she was supposed to wait until her assistant got there. But we kept walking down the beat-up, old walkway. By the time we got to the end, the cab was pulling up. I looked back at the old, four-story building and remembered how it had held me captive for weeks. I wanted to erase it all from my mind, but I knew that I never would.

CHAPTER 17

Detroit

As we entered the city, the captain gave us a weather report and announced that we were landing in Detroit. Joy, Sue, and I all looked at each other and laughed. We were happy to hear the captain say, "Detroit," because the last time we were on a plane, we had been asleep when the plane landed, and we ended up in Baltimore. The other passengers wondered what was so funny, but they didn't know that it was a personal joke among us. Ms. Lynn didn't see the humor either. I thought, Ms. Lynn, you don't think its funny now, but we didn't think it was funny in Baltimore.

When the plane landed, we got off and walked down the long walkway to the terminal. I stayed behind; I wanted the family to reunite first and then I'd say Hi to Jay. As soon as we got into the lobby I saw Jay—the best looking guy in the entire room. I wanted to run over and hug and kiss him, but I managed to control myself enough to wait until he'd seen and greeted his family first. When they saw Jay and his uncles across the room, they went over and hugged and kissed them, and they talked for a while. I sat on one of the lobby chairs across the room, and waited until they were done.

Then I saw Jay looking around. The look in his eyes let me know that he'd missed me and wanted to see me. The lobby was full, but I managed to walk up behind Jay and put my hand into his. He squeezed it tight; then he turned around and gave me a kiss that warmed my body like it did "that night" in his room. I knew then that I was addicted to his touch, his kiss, and his love. I had to have a "dose of Jay" every day, I thought, from now on. I could never go back to Miami. It was a long way home, and I thought that if I went back, I'd never be happy without Jay. Lenny said that we should go down to baggage claim and that he'd drive the car around and meet us at the door.

After we kissed, Jay wanted to know how I was. "Hi, Babe. I'm glad to see you," Jay said, as we walked behind everyone to the baggage claim area.

"Hey Jay, good to see you too." "Are you alright?" Jay asked.

"I'm a little confused, but I'm OK."

"Look. I'm sorry for what my mother did to all of you, and I guess you already know that Bee has issues. We laughed about it and kept walking to the baggage claim. Ms. Lynn looked back and gave me a look that sent chills down my back. I stopped laughing and kept my eye on her. She seemed to be mad at me all the time after that; she wasn't the Ms. Lynn I knew before we left Miami.

When we got downstairs, Jim was already there and had paid the porter to get our bags as we showed them to him; he put them on a cart and then into the car. When we got outside, Joy, Sue and Ms. Lynn got into the back seat, and Jim got in the front with Lenny. I looked at Jay, and he said, "I thought we'd spend a little time together before we got to the house, so I drove Jim's car to the airport for us."

"Good," I said. "I was wondering if we'd get some personal time together tonight."

"Louise, I've missed you so much, and when they told me that you were gone, I just about lost my mind."

"I'm sorry, Jay. I should have called you; I just wanted to be with you." Jay opened the door of the car, and I got in. I saw that Jay had some tapes ready to play. He went around and got in. Once he was behind the wheel, the music started, and he sang, "My Girl" by the Temptations to me and then "La-La Means I Love You."

Jay left the parking lot and pulled onto the freeway. He'd already told Lenny that we'd meet them at the house later, and that he was going to show me a little of the city. When we got off of the freeway, Jay turned down a very busy street where all types of people were walking around at night, doing all kind of strange things.

We stopped at a traffic light, and while we were sitting there, a female walked up to the car and flashed opened her jacket! She didn't have a bra or a t-shirt on! She looked at us and said, "Anybody want to trade? I'm your trick for $10.00."

"No! and get away from my car." Jay raced his engine. I didn't know what was going on. I'd never seen anything like that before. She looked about Lisa's age, and life hadn't treated her too kindly either.

"Well, what about her?" she said, pointing her finger at me. I almost choked.

The light turned green, and Jay took off."

"Jay, what kind of trick did the lady want to do?" I wanted to know. Jay started to laugh, and I couldn't understand what was so funny. What could she do at a traffic light at night, stand on her head?

"Don't worry about it, Babe. Detroit is a fast city, and you have a lot to learn. If you don't know who you are or what you're doing, this city will swallow you up." We turned another corner, and Jay drove about two blocks down the street. We slowed down as Jay started talking to some guys in front of what looked like a nightclub. They waved at Jay, and he waved back and gave them a thumbs-up.

"Hey, Man, everything alright?" Jay asked, as he hung over the side of the window.

"Yeah, Man, everything's cool," and the guy gave Jay a thumbs-up in return. "You know these guys? Who are they?" I asked.

"This is Lenny and Jim's night club, and those guys are the bouncer and watchman. They work for them."

"Are we going in now?" I asked, getting myself freshened up in the mirror. "No, Louise, not tonight. I just wanted to let you see The Club. Everyone is waiting for us at the house too." Jay drove a little further down the street, and then he showed me a large building. That's the Twenty Grand Club. Jim and Lenny used to hang out there, back in their day. Jay said that he'd give me a real tour of the city the next day, and he pulled back onto the freeway. We drove for about half an hour, and we got off again.

Jay turned into a neighborhood that was beautiful. It had manicured lawns, nicely painted houses, and was very quiet. I could tell it was an upper, middle- class neighborhood. When we walked inside, the house looked like a well-kept, bachelor's house. There were photos of entertainers and some photos of Jim with the entertainers. I looked at one picture of Jim and David Ruffin, one of the Motown Temptations, standing at the bar together at The Club. I was so excited; I picked the picture up and rushed over to show it to Jay. He called Jim over to see how excited I was.

"Hey Miami, you like that picture, huh?" Jim asked me with his Hennessey clinking in his glass. No matter what your name was, Jim had a reason for giving you another name. He called me, Miami, and he called Jay, Miami Slim. Still excited, I gave Jim a big hug.

"Yes, I actually know someone that really knows David Ruffin." "That's right, you know somebody when you know Diamond Jim!"

Jim was full of himself that night. He said he called me Miami because he could never remember my name. And when Jay first got to Detroit, all he talked about was his girl in Miami, until he started calling Jay, Miami Slim. So I had to get used to it. "When will David Rufflin be a guest of yours again, Jim?"

"Well, Miami, you're in luck; David is going to be our surprise entertainment tomorrow night." I was so happy; I was just like a kid. I was going to see him in person. After that we all sat around, talked, had drinks and listened to music.

It was getting late, and I still had not called Mama. Jay must have been thinking about that call too. He came over to me and asked if I was ready to make the call yet. I said, yes I was ready. We went into Jay's room. I told Jay to close the door to block out all the noise. "We wouldn't want your parents to think that you're having any fun," Jay teased. I got up enough nerve to make the call. The phone rang.

"Hello."

"Hi, Bobbie; it's me. Let me speak to Mama."

"Daddy took her to a party. Where are you? How are you? When are you coming back home?" Bobbie was excited to hear from me, and I was glad to hear her voice too. We'd missed each other, but things had changed.

"I don't know. Look, I'll call you back." I hung up the phone, and I wanted to cry. Jay knew I needed to be alone for awhile, so he went out of the room. When he came back in, he comforted me. Jay said if I wanted him to take me back home, that he would, whenever I was ready. And he'd still loved me. As we walked back out to the party, Ms. Lynn and the girls were heading into Jay's room. That's where we girls were going to sleep; I went back into the room too.

and a blanket. I guess Joy and Sue went right to sleep, but I stayed up most of the night thinking about Jay. When I did fall off to sleep, I woke up crying. After tossing and turning the whole night through, I got up early the next morning. I showered and got dressed before the others got up, so that I could take my time. I wanted to look my best for Jay. When I opened the room's door, Jay was already showered and dressed; he'd even folded his blanket and put it away with his pillow.

"Good morning, Babe, did you sleep well?" Jay asked, with an early-morning, sexy smile.

"Well, I had a good rest, but I couldn't sleep that long. I was too excited." "Well, if I know my sisters, they'll sleep til noon, no matter what happens." "Yeah, they always had a hard time getting up when we were in Baltimore." "Louise, I really wish you'd forget about Baltimore, and I can't tell you how sorry I am about what Bee did."

"Jay, it's OK. I don't want to forget about Baltimore. It was a good experience for me; I learned a lot. Now, what do you have planned for today?"

"I'm going to take you to breakfast, and then we're going to tour the city." "Sounds like a plan to me." I got my purse and was ready to go. We got into the car, and Jay turned on the radio, and we sang along with every song that came on. He finally stopped in front of a store-front restaurant; we went inside and took a seat at a front table. Jay said that the service was faster in that section. Jay looked at the menu to see what he wanted. I didn't have to; I'd already gotten a whiff of their bacon and waffles. The waitress took our order.

came over to our table. They stood over our table like two, tall trees. They were neatly dressed in colorful dashikis, and their afros were neatly trimmed and looked almost as good as Jay's. "What's up Jay?" they said with a bright smile.

"Everything is everything." Whatever that meant. "Man, is this your lady?"

"Yeah, Man, this is the young lady I was telling you about from Miami." "Good morning, Miss. How are you?"

"I'm fine, thank you."

One guy went to the counter to place an order, but the other one stayed in our faces, smiling. Jay soon got annoyed with him. "Man, what do you want?" Jay demanded, with fire in his eyes.

"OK, Man, I get the message," as he backed away from the table. "Later, Man."

"OK, see you at work tonight, Jay."

Just before the waitress came back to the table with our food, a man came and stood beside our table. He looked scared and as if he was in a hurry. He wanted to sell Jay a Rolex watch for fifty dollars. Jay said that the watch was no fake, but that the guy was a junky. He'd either stolen it or robbed someone and taken it off of them. Whoever bought that watch was going to jail or hell if the person saw their watch.

We finally got our breakfast. We ate and headed over to The Club. Jay had a couple of things he said he had to do. As we walked out to the car, I looked at Jay and realized that I'd missed him more than I thought. I missed Mama too, but I'd rather be here than go back to Miami. I kept thinking, when I do talk to my parents, I'll tell them that I'm not coming home. Jay saw that I was deep in thought.

"Louise, what's wrong, why are you so quiet?"

"I'm just thinking about that phone call I have to make." "Have you made up your mind what you're going to do?"

"Yes, I'm going to stay here with you." I knew that if I ever went back, that it'd never be the same. I was my own woman, and I'd better start acting like it.

By the time we reached The Club, it was already ten-thirty. We got out of the car and went in. The cleaning guys had all the doors open. They said that they had to air the place out. They were cleaning tables, walls and the floors, getting ready for that night. As we walked through The Club, I saw new posters hanging up that read, "Surprise Entertainment for Tonight. Guess Who?" I was glad that I knew who it was; Jim had already told me that he was going to have David Ruffin as a guest. "Jay! Look at this poster; I know who it is!" Jay smiled at my excitement.

"Yeah, Babe. David's going to be a guest at our VIP table tonight too. I'll pick you up tonight after I get off."

"What time would that be, Jay?"

"It'll be about eleven, OK?" Jay had really gone to The Club that morning because he had to take care of the books, and I got to see the inside of The Club in the process, before they opened. Jay went to his office, and I wandered around The Club. Everything looked great. The blue and silver tables and chairs were cleaned and shining, and the blue floors with diamond designs all over it were polished perfectly. They had all of the exit doors open, and the sunlight was beaming. There wasn't any music or any people. Everything smelled fresh and clean. It was hard to imagine that it was a night club. My last memory of a night club was a smoke-filled room with a crowded, dance floor, good music, and someone groping my body parts as I moved through the crowd.

Jay finished his bookkeeping, and we got in the car and headed home. When we got there, Lenny had left a message that read: I'm taking Bee and the girls out to lunch, and we are going sightseeing. See you when we get back. When we realized that we were alone, Jay kissed me. I'd almost forgotten how his kisses heated me up and made me want more of him. I remembered that the last time we made love, was also my first time.

I was nervous and didn't know what to do. I couldn't remember if Jay took off my clothes the last time or if I did; some of that night was a fog. Jay kissed me again and again. We went into the day-room and sat on the bed. I loved Jay, but I was still a bit nervous, "Jay I don't know," I said. I remembered having some pain that night, but I still wanted to do it, because it was a nice pain, if there is such a thing. I can't explain it, but I said, yes, I wanted more.

Jay moved smooth and easy. He knew that I was nervous. He held me and said, "Don't worry, Babe. I'll talk you through it." After Jay pushed all the right buttons, our bodies fell into the right motion, and we loved each other until our bodies were wet with sweat.

We got up, showered and got dressed. Jay was late for work, and I had to get everything cleaned up before everyone got back home. By three o'clock a car drove up in front of the house; it was Ms. Lynn and the girls. I was sitting on the couch watching TV. Lenny came in, "Jay went to work, huh Louise?"

"Yeah, he's gone," I said, trying not to look anyone in the eyes. "I thought he'd stay home because you were here."

"No! He told me this morning that he was going to work."

The phone ranged and Lenny answered it. "Who called?" Ms. Lynn asked.

"It was Jim. He wants you to call the caterer and order some meat platters; we're going to have an after-party tonight when we leave The Club. A new club had opened on the east side. Tammi Terrell, a background singer for James Brown, was performing there. Jim invited her and Marvin Gaye to the party after she finished her last show. Ms. Lynn got on the phone and called the caterers; she also ordered flowers and extras to make sure everything was ready for that night. There was never a dull moment at this place. There were parties and people around all the time, and now I was a part of it.

Although it was hard getting used to my new-found freedom, I knew I would. I'd lived under Daddy's Rules for so long; it was hard for me to "get out of line." And even though Mama wasn't there, it still felt like I needed someone to tell me what I should and should not do. Now I made my own decisions, and I was responsible for my own mistakes.

The evening rolled around before we realized it. Ms. Lynn had the tables decorated and everything set-up and looking nice. She had the meat platters, side dishes, and drinks lined up for the occasion. Joy and Sue had gone back out to shop for new outfits.

When they came in I was excited to see their outfits, but Joy said that she didn't want anyone to see what she was going to wear to the party until that night. Joy was a little pissed off with me, because I was doing as I pleased, the way she used to do when we were back in Miami. She was on lock-down and couldn't get out, so she blamed me.

I thought that maybe I should tell her to be thankful that she had a family that cared about her. I wished mine was there, although I hadn't told them how much I loved them when I was home. Sure

I was having fun with my new freedom, but sometimes even when I laughed, I was sad inside. I often asked myself, why not just go back home? My excuse would be, "It's a long way home, and I can't turn back now."

I overlooked Joy's anger and started getting dressed. It wasn't time to go to The Club yet, but we were having house guests, and I had to be dressed for the occasion. I showered and put on my red and gold bell-bottom jumpsuit, my big hoop earrings, and my new gold bangles. I even pulled the hot comb through my afro to make it look fuller. I checked myself out in the mirror, and I was truly all together and ready to take on the night. I went into the living room to play some of my favorite songs. The phone rang, and the person on the other end wanted to talk to Jim. They were excited.

"Jim, Jim. The phone is for you." I shook Jim as hard as I could; he slept hard whenever he did go to sleep.

"Who is it?" Jim asked.

"I don't know; it's someone from The Club." I answered.

"OK, tell them to hold on." I went back to the phone to tell the person that Jim was coming, and I could hear the music and laughter in the background. I could hardly wait until Jay got home, so that we could get down there. Jim came in and I handed him the phone. "Hello, who is this?" Jim asked in a still sleepy voice.

"It's Troy, Man."

Jim seemed agitated that someone had called while he was sleeping. "Why are you calling me now? It's only eleven." Troy talked loud; I could hear everything he said from where I was sitting on the couch.

"Man, you need to come down here right now. Everything's rolling, and you need to come and make a pick-up before the late crowd start coming in." The Club was always packed when the late crowd came in because they had live entertainment after twelve.

"Can't you put it in the safe?"

"The safe is full. You know that Lenny doesn't want this kind of money left in the office." Someone always picked up the overflow money when they had a good night.

"OK, I'll get dressed and cruise on down there," Jim offered. "OK, Man."

"OK, later." Jim got dressed in his dark green and gold pin-stripped, three- piece suit with a gold shirt and cuff links that spelled J-I-M. I could never get used to the way Jim dressed. Sometimes he looked nice, and sometimes he looked like a fool. When he came out of the room, he greeted everyone and headed for the door. He walked outside and got into his green Eldorodo and backed out of the driveway.

The young guys across the street saw Jim. They stopped what they were doing and walked to the edge of their yard and called out all together, "Diamond Jim, what's up!" as they waved at him. (They always talked about how cool Jim was.)

"Nothing, Brother," he answered as he drove off waving his arm in the air. When Diamond Jim got to The Club, Jay had already stopped there and picked up the money before he went home. They also gave Jay the money from the gambling table. So Jim was free to stay at The Club just in case some of the celebrities came early.

By the time Jay got to the house, it was already 1:30 AM, and I had been looking out of the window every ten minutes to see if he had come yet. I'd heard Lenny talking to Jay earlier that evening on the phone. That's when I realized that Jay was at The Club. I had already said to myself, Jay will call and tell me that he is at The Club and had to stay there because of the crowd, which meant I couldn't go to The Club. But he didn't. Jay knew how much being there that night meant to me. The door opened, and it was Jay. When he came in, he walked straight to the back room. I tried calling out to him, "Hi, Jay." But the music was too loud; he kept on walking. I pushed past the crowd, and just as I got to the door, he closed it in my face.

Out the corner of my eyes I could see two guys standing there laughing and saying, "That's right, Honey, make him let you in." I turned to see who they were, and Lenny came up. The two guys hurried back into the living room.

"What was that all about Lenny?" I asked.

"Jay made a pick-up when he stopped at The Club. I believe those two clowns were going to try something real stupid tonight," Lenny answered.

"I just wanted to say, hello, and tell him that I was ready to go."

"I know, Louise, but if we're entertaining, and Jay or Jim goes directly to the backroom, let them do what they have to do. You can catch them on their way out, OK?"

I said, "OK," but Lenny's little talk made me realize that what Jay had told me earlier was true. Detroit was a fast city. I had to be on my toes all the time. Jay came out of the room about thirty minutes later. He was in a good mood, singing and popping his fingers. I could see him from the kitchen. He was looking around for me and calling my name. I went over to greet him, and he took my hand and pulled me out on the dance floor. We danced to "My Girl" by the Temptations. Everyone was watching us dance and enjoy ourselves.

I looked at Lenny, and he gave me thumbs up. I'd thought Lenny didn't like me. I'd heard him tell one of his friends the first night we'd come in from Baltimore, that I'd be like a fish out of water in Detroit, and that maybe Jay should throw me back, because I was jail bait anyway. I didn't know what he meant by that, but at that moment, I thought he felt differently. The music stopped, and Jay asked me as we walked to the front door, "Are you having a good time?"

"Yes, but I'd have a better time, if we were at The Club." "OK, then let's go."

"I'll get my purse." When I got back, Jay had asked one of his friends to go out to his car and bring in a large box. They gave me the box, and I opened it. Jay had bought me a beautiful, winter coat. It had already gotten cold outside. I'd forgotten that their winters weren't like Miami's weather. It was October and cold already. Once we got outside, I was glad that Jay had bought me a coat.

Jay told Lenny and the other guys that we were leaving, while I waited by the door. When Jay was done, we walked out to his car. Jay was always driving Jim's car, so I had not realized that the red and white Lincoln sitting in the garage was Jay's car. It had the gangster, white walls and tinted windows. We got in and Jay turned on the heater, and then the radio, and Aretha Franklin was singing "Chain of Fools." Jay backed out, and we were headed for the freeway with Aretha thumping all the way there.

CHAPTER 18

A Night Out in Motown

We got to The Club in about forty-five minutes. Jay pulled up in front. It looked different at night. It had a blue and white canopy out front that ran from the building to the public sidewalk. On top of the building it read, "The Club." It looked real classy. Jay had parked right in the street. We got out, and one of the guys that was standing out front came and drove the car away and parked it. When we walked inside, I started to feel a little uneasy because of the way some of the females were looking at Jay and calling to him.

"Do you know these women?" I asked Jay. I was mad and jealous, and I let him know it.

"Yeah, I know all of them, but not personally." "And what does that mean?" I asked.

"It means that they are all regulars. They come down here every night looking for free drinks, some conversation, and even sex. Don't worry, Babe. They know my limit has always been a little conversation and maybe a free drink."

I understood what Jay was telling me; he had to at least be sociable with the clientele. I may have been young, but I was learning fast.

We walked up front to the V-I-P Section, and anybody who was somebody was permitted to sit at that table. When we got to our reserved table, we sat down, and everyone introduced themselves. The lady that sat on my left was beautiful. She had smooth, black skin, silky shoulder-length hair, and she was small and petite. She said her name was Jackie and that she was a dancer. Jay interrupted to ask me if I wanted a drink.

"I'll have a vodka and orange juice." I answered. "You want some smokes too, Babe?"

"Oh, yes, get me a pack of Kools." I was just learning to smoke, but Jay knew it made me feel more grown up if he asked about the cigarettes anyway."

"I thought you switched to Salem's," he said. I'd forgotten that the last time I tried to smoke one of Jay's Kools, I'd almost choked to death. They were so strong they could put hair on your chest. They all made me dizzy, but I was determined to smoke.

Jay and Diamond Jim were busy watching the door and discussing some business matters. Jackie said that she was going to the Ladies Room. It was time for me to release some of the vodka I'd put down, so I went too. When I came out of the bathroom stall, Jackie was checking her make-up. I washed my hands and checked mine too. When we got back, Jackie put her purse down and walked over to the bar. Jay asked, "Where did you two go?"

"We went to the Ladies Room." I thought it was a little strange that Jay would be asking me where I went, but I just let it go.

Then Jay leaned over and said, "Jackie's a man." At first I thought I didn't hear him right.

"What?" Jay pointed in Jackie's direction and nodded his head. "Jackie-is-a-man?" I could hardly believe my ears. bathroom with is a man."

"But look at her, she's so beautiful. How could she be a man?"

"I know that's what a lot of men think too, until they discover her little secret."

I fixed myself another drink, more vodka than juice that time. It was my last drink that night, and my tongue felt so thick and heavy I could hardly talk. When Jackie came back to the table, she was very talkative and I hung onto her every word, trying to see if she even sounded like a man. But her voice was softer and more tender than mine, and she moved more graceful than any female at the table. I couldn't take my eyes off her.

Jay tried to take my attention away from Jackie. He tapped my shoulder and said, "Louise, here comes David."

"David? David who?" Everyone sitting at the table looked at me, and I looked at Jackie. I was in bad shape, tipsy and dizzy.

"It's David Ruffin. He's coming over here now," Jackie informed me.

When he got to the table, Diamond Jim stood up to greet him, and everyone in the front section began to clap and cheer. David Ruffin sat down next to Jay. He said good evening to everyone, and he and Jay gave each other a manly hug. "S-o, Miami Slim, it's been a while since I've seen you," David said to Jay.

"Yeah, Man, I had to have my lady with me."

"Hello, Miss Miami. Diamond Jim told me a lot about you today when we talked."

for me to talk. He grinned back, and Jay asked me to dance. He wanted to get me away from the table. He knew that I'd had too much to drink, and he didn't want to let me make a fool of myself. Jay told David and the others to excuse us. The Delfonics sounded good as we danced into the crowd. "Didn't I Blow Your Mind This Time" was playing. I was dancing to Jay's step, but I saw two of him. He took me outside to get some fresh air. We talked about how I'd let myself get tipsy, and how I'd let the alcohol control me. I remembered how he'd lectured Joy about alcohol, and now Jay sounded like my big brother, I thought. But I knew he was right.

When we got back inside, Jay said that he had to check on something in his office. When we got to the office, he told me to have a seat until he got back from the bar. He needed to get their receipts. Jay's office only had a safe, a desk, a chair and a folding cart. I sat at Jay's desk for awhile, but he took so long I thought I'd lie down on the cart until he got back. I went to sleep.

When I opened my eyes again, Jay was waking me up to take me home. After I'd gotten myself together and collected my thoughts, I remembered the show. I'd missed the show! I wanted to wring Jay's neck. He'd let me sleep through the show. But my head was hurting so bad, all I wanted was to go home and get into bed. When we got ready to leave, I told Jay that I had to go to the Ladies Room. He said, OK, and that he'd meet me by the front door. He had to stuff the rest of the money into the suitcase. They turned over so much money that night that Lenny told the pick-up guy to leave it in the safe until it was time to close up.

When I opened the door, everyone was gone except the cleaning guys. They had the bright lights on, and cups, napkins, cigarettes and ash trays were all over the tables, and the chairs pulled out from the tables made it look like they'd had an 80% off sale at Sears. Jay told the guys to hurry up—he'd made the pick-up and was leaving.

As we were going, Jackie opened the door. She was bleeding. Her face and arms were covered with blood. She turned around and shut the door, going back outside. We could hear her screaming, "Lock the doors and call the cops. They're going to rob you!" At that moment, I realized that everyone in the room had pulled out a gun except me. They locked the doors, and I called the cops. Then there was silence.... nothing.... then we heard two gunshots, and Jackie screamed again. Two of the guys aimed their guns, opened the door and went outside. They could see the two guys running away, and Jackie was on the ground, lying in a puddle of blood.

I screamed. I thought she was dead. But she held her head up and said, "It's Big Man and Junior." She closed her eyes.

I screamed again, "Oh, no, they've killed Jackie!"

The rescue squad was there before we knew it. They worked on Jackie and put her in their rescue truck and drove away. The police had some questions they needed answered. They told me to sit at the table in the corner and wait for them. As I waited, I couldn't help but think about Jackie's secret. They're going to take off her clothes, and they'll know. They'll know that Jackie is a man. I had to make myself stop thinking like that. I should have been praying for Jackie's life, not thinking about her secret.

The cops came over to my table, and Jay came over with them. He told the police that I really didn't see anything because I had been in the Ladies Room. We didn't want them to know that I was not yet eighteen. I confirmed that I'd not seen anything and was ready to get out of there. They closed up The Club that night just the way it was.

CHAPTER 19

Time for a Change

Sunday morning I got up and went into the living room. Jay and his uncles were in the dining room reading the newspaper. The news about The Club's attempted robbery and shooting was all over the paper. They said that Jackie was still critical, but that she'd make it. The news about her secret was also out. They had a full page write-up on it: "Jackie Dawsen aka Jack Dawsen." The paper talked about Jackie's dancing career as a male and as a female. I felt bad for Jackie, I wanted to cry for her, but there wasn't anything I could do.

The cops had also found the robbers. It was Big Man and Junior! After they tried to rob The Club that night, they had tried to break into someone's home. Junior got shot in the chest, and Big Man tried to drop him off at the ER and leave him there, but someone noticed him and called security. They took Junior inside the emergency room, and they took Big Man to jail.

When Ms. Lynn came out of the kitchen, she was mad at all of us. She said that I didn't need to be around all of that drama. I needed to sign up for some type of class or something, and that Jay should keep me out of that night club. I didn't know what to say. "Jay, you know that girl is too young for that kind of night life." Ms. Lynn had no idea of what kind of night life her own baby girl was living back in Miami, but I didn't say anything.

"Bee, you took a minor out of the state and away from her parents, and now you're worried about a night club? Look what you did to my two sisters in Baltimore." Ms. Lynn ran out of the room crying; she always got angry if any one talked about Baltimore.

We all went to the hospital that day. Jay and I rode in his car. He asked me what type of career I had in mind before his mom took me away. I said I wanted to be a lifetime student at the Jay Academy. We both laughed and agreed to discuss it later.

CHAPTER 20

Jackie Dawsen

When we got to the hospital, we went to the front desk. They told us that J. Dawsen was in ICU. We went upstairs, and we saw Jackie before she saw us. She was crying, and it looked like she was talking to herself. But when we got closer, we stood in the doorway and heard Jackie praying and thanking God that she was still alive.

Jackie looked so different to me. Her hair was cut to about an inch, and she didn't have on any make-up. But I could see a five o'clock shadow showing on her face, and her voice wasn't as soft and silky as it was the night I met her at The Club. Even when Jackie had screamed that night at The Club, she had sounded like a lady. But not this day.

Diamond Jim told Jackie that when she felt better, she could go to The Club any time she wanted to, and anything she wanted would be free. Jackie thanked Jim, and then she told him and everyone in the room that she was saved, and that she wouldn't be back in The Club any more. The room was silent for about three minutes. No one knew what to say.

Then the nurse came in, and she said that there were too many visitors in the room and that Mr. Dawsen needed his rest. Jim looked at the nurse and told her that he liked her. He grabbed her hand and kissed it, and said that she was very pretty. He asked her if she wanted to work for him. The nurse laughed and said, "Diamond Jim, I already know about that chain of fools you have working for you." We laughed again, and so did Jackie. It was good seeing her smile. She'd been looking so sad, so different, and so not the person I'd met that night at The Club. The nurse tried to quiet us down and wave us out the door. We left Jack to talk to the nurse.

CHAPTER 21

News about Junior

Too much was going on in our house on Cherry Lawn. They were single men, and their home evolved around their night life. Ms. Lynn said that the company they entertained was too fast for her daughters. They were bad examples for us, and we needed to move.

Troy came in the door and told Jay that the night of the robbery, Big Man and Junior had come to the house to rob everyone. They told Peanut that Lenny was watching and following them too closely. Peanut said that when Jay had come home, he hadn't stopped—he'd gone straight to the back room. So they got themselves a drink and left.

Troy also told us that Junior had died from his gunshot wounds. When Troy left, we all agreed that the four of us females would get an apartment the next week.

CHAPTER 22

Moving On

We found an apartment on the other side of town. It was located on Livernois and Epworth. The neighborhood was nice and quiet, and we loved it. We moved in and got settled in a few weeks. I got a letter from the Man Power Division where I'd applied for the nursing program. I was accepted and expected to show up in two weeks with my white uniform and an anatomy book. I was very excited; I was doing something responsible for my future.

I'd been in nursing school six weeks, and everything was going fine. One morning I got up to get dressed. I went into the bathroom and started to brush my teeth. I felt like throwing up, then I got dizzy, and I fell out on the bathroom floor. Joy must have heard me when I fell because when I woke up, I was in bed, and Ms. Lynn had a cold washcloth on my head.

Ms. Lynn called for Jay to come over. When he got there, she told him what had happened that morning. She told Jay to take me to Dr. Harper for an exam. Jay and I had an idea what had happened, but neither of us would say anything—we just left. When we got to Dr. Harper's office, Jay told the receptionist what'd happened, and I went and sat down. I was still feeling kind of sick. The nurse told me to go into the exam room. The doctor came in and examined me. Then he asked me some questions and went back out.

The nurse came in and got some blood and urine from me. Then she went back out. When they were finished with me, the doctor told me that I was pregnant. I had to sit down for a few minutes and process what he'd said. "Pregnant?" I asked, "As in, I'm going to have a baby?" Jay came in while I was sitting there, and I told him the news. It seemed as though Jay wanted to smile, but he looked at me and didn't know how I'd taken the news. We walked out of the office without talking. I was shocked, confused and afraid.

"Louise, how do you feel about the news?" Jay asked.

"I don't know," I answered, as I peeled the nail polish from my nails. "Babe, I love you."

"I love you too, Jay."

"Look at that, our love is so strong we've created a new life."

"Yeah, we did, huh?" I thought about my older sister Anne having a baby so young, and how Daddy's Rules had gotten started. What would Daddy have to say about this situation?

Then I could hear Jay calling me, "Louise, Louise, what's the matter? Aren't you happy about the news?"

"I'm afraid. But I'm happy." The news really blew my mind. "Now there is something we have to do."

"What's that?"

"We need to call your mother."

"No!! We can't. We can't tell Mama! I can't call her, not now." What was wrong with Jay, I thought, is he trying to get me in trouble? My childlike mentality had come back. I'd forgotten that I was supposed to be a grown woman and responsible for my own actions, until Jay reminded me.

Then he tried to comfort me, "Louise we have to do this, I'll even tell her that it's all my fault."

"But what if she wants to put you in jail?"

"Trust me, Babe. We need to call her tonight." We agreed to call Mama that night. When Jay dropped me off, he said that he was going over to Lenny's house to tell everyone that he was a father, and he'd be right back.

Two hours later, Jay came back with three suitcases and boxes. Jay said that he was moving in. When Ms. Lynn saw Jay's bags and boxes, she came out of her room. Then she heard Jay tell me that he was moving in and that we were going to be roommates. I was so happy I could cry, but the look on Ms. Lynn's face told us that she didn't like Jay's idea. "Just what do you think you're doing?" Ms. Lynn asked, standing over Jay's bags with her hands on her hips.

"What does it look like, Bee? I'm moving in with my lady. I'm a father now." "Well, that does not mean you have to move in with her," she shouted, throwing her hands up in the air.

"Yes, it does Bee. I'm not going to be like my father. I won't abandon my kid."

"You're talking crazy, Jay. I don't want to hear it." Jay was mad, and I was hurt. I knew then that Ms. Lynn really didn't care about me.

"No, I'm not crazy. I love Louise, and she's going to have my kid, and I'm going to take care of her," Jay insisted.

Ms. Lynn had been talking about me just as if I wasn't even standing in the room, and it hurt me that she felt the way she did about me. Ms. Lynn thought that once Jay found out that I was pregnant, he'd stay away from me, but she was wrong. Jay told Ms. Lynn that if she didn't like him moving in with me so that he could take care of me, that we'd get our own apartment, and she'd have this one all to herself. Ms. Lynn calmed down, and they talked about the house expenses. Jay said he'd pay the rent and gas and take care of me. And Ms. Lynn said she'd pay lights and water and take care of Joy and Sue.

Later that night we called Mama. Jay placed the call around 8 o'clock. The phone rang, and someone picked up. It sounded like

Mama, "Hello." There was silence for about ten seconds—I was afraid to talk.

"Hello, Mama? This is your daughter, Louise." When I heard Mama's voice, I cried, and so did Mama. She cried so hard, I couldn't understand anything she was saying, but I still tried to talk to her. "Hello, Mama. Please don't cry. I love you, and I'm sorry."

Mama finally stopped crying long enough to talk to me. "Hello, Louise! Baby, are you alright?" Mama's shaky voice asked between sniffles.

"Yea, Mama, I'm alright," I answered with an even more shaky voice.

"When are you coming home, Baby? Since you've been gone, I've been sick. I have high blood pressure now. Girl, you scared me so bad I thought I was going to die." When Mama told me that, I started to cry uncontrollably. Jay took the phone from me and got on himself. I sat on the bed next to Jay while he talked. I could hear Mama's voice on the phone cussing Jay for everything she could think of. Mama didn't say bad words very often, but when she got on you, it hurt deep down in your soul. Jay understood Mama's anger; he didn't even try to defend himself.

Then Jay talked to Daddy. I was surprised, but they had a civil conversation. They made a plan so Mama could fly to Detroit, and they said that they'd talk later. When Jay hung up the phone, I was still crying. Ms. Lynn said that I should stop crying so much, it wasn't good for the baby. We closed the door, and Jay tried to comfort me.

The phone rang. I thought, oh, no, Mama was calling back to try to make me go back home. But when Ms. Lynn answered, it was her younger brother. He'd gotten into some serious trouble and needed to come to Detroit for awhile. Ms. Lynn came to our room to ask Jay if it was OK with him for her brother to stay with us for awhile. Ms. Lynn knew that Jay and her brother Roy didn't get along well, but Jay said, OK, anyway.

By November 1, st Mama made a trip to Detroit. Her visit was very resourceful. She and I made peace with each other, and Jay and I got married. Even though Mama and Ms. Lynn had some strong words for each other, they managed to control themselves until Mama's visit was over. Maybe they'd be able to forgive each other for what they said and realize that they couldn't control our lives, I hoped.

By November 15, Th Ms. Lynn's brother was able to leave the State of Florida and travel to Detroit. Roy had been in jail and was on probation. He had been in and out of jail for drugs, robbery, and disturbing the peace. He came to live with us for a little while. Jay knew that his sister Joy and his uncle Roy were very close when they were in Miami, before Roy went to jail. They sat around talking for hours that night Roy first got in. I learned that Roy had started Joy smoking and drinking when she was twelve. Jay had been in Viet Nam, and Ms. Lynn was working all the time.

Hours went by as the two of them talked about old times. They laughed about the things they used to do, but Ms. Lynn didn't think it was so funny. Roy had given Her Baby alcohol and had started her smoking, when she'd left him to look after Joy. Ms. Lynn was crying when Jay came into the room. He'd already heard what was going on. Jay gave Roy some house rules: he told Roy what he could and could not do and what time he had to be in the house. Jay told Roy that if he didn't like it, to let him know, and he'd personally pay for his ticket back to Miami. Roy agreed, and we all cleaned up everything and went to bed.

CHAPTER 23

Thanksgiving Day at Lenny's

Roy was doing just great. Three weeks had passed, and there was no trouble from him, and no sign of him taking drugs. Roy helped out around the house, and he even went to the store for us.

The next Thursday was Thanksgiving, and Lenny was having a big Thanksgiving Dinner, we were all invited. I was so glad to have a chance to get out of the house. I'd been in bed most of the time with morning sickness, so I stayed in the house all the time. The pregnancy didn't seem to be going very well for me, I thought.

On Thanksgiving Day, we all went over to Lenny's house for dinner. When we got there, they were sitting around and watching the football games in the living room and in the family room. They were also playing cards, having drinks, and listening to music. We were all having a great time when the housekeeper came in and informed us that the dinner would be ready in a few minutes. She'd catered in the turkey and ham, but she had prepared the veggies and other side dishes for the meal herself. Everything looked beautiful, and Bertha, the housekeeper, was a great hostess.

Jay said that Bertha and Lenny were undercover lovers. She was married, and Lenny had two other women, and they were all trying to keep Lenny's attention. Even though they all knew about each other, Jay said that Lenny told them that they had to share him, but he made each of them think that she was really the special one.

I was going to the bathroom when the doorbell rang, so I told Bertha that I'd answer the door. When I opened the door, it was Jackie/Jack standing there, smiling. At first I didn't know who the little guy was. Then he smiled and said, "Hey, Little Lady, I see you've been busy." I smiled and looked closer, and realized that it was Jackie. She had beautiful dimples, and she wore them even better as a man. Jackie was cute, as a man. I managed to stop staring at him long enough to let him in.

He said that he wasn't going to stay long, but that he'd just come by because they'd invited him, and he wanted to tell everyone, Happy Thanksgiving. Jack's left arm didn't move; he kept it in a bent position all of the time. He said that he was taking physical therapy, and when his arm was completely healed, he was going back on the stage to dance, in New York.

I had the urge to use the restroom again, but when I got to the bathroom door, it was closed. I knocked, and there was no answer. I tried to push the door open, but it felt as though someone was pushing it back shut. I didn't know what was going on in there. "Hello, is anyone in there?" I asked. No answer. "Hello, are you alright in there?" I asked again. Still no answer.

I pushed the door open as hard as I could, and I saw Roy in there on the floor. I could see blood all over his shirt. I screamed for someone to go in and get him out of there. Roy was lying across the small bathroom floor, and his feet were pressing against the door. Jay managed to push the door hard enough to open it. They sat Roy up against the bathtub and tried to see where the blood was coming from. Then Jay noticed a small syringe sticking out of Roy's arm. "Dope!"

Jay said, "This clown's been shooting up dope." Roy's head went back, and his eyes were showing only the whites.

Ms. Lynn was crying. She wanted to call the rescue squad when she saw the white foam coming from Roy's mouth. Diamond Jim said, "Get-him-out-of- here!" Jim said that they didn't want any attention drawn to their house involving drugs because they entertained celebrities. Jim wanted Roy out of the house, but Mickey, a known drug dealer, was used to that happening to junkies. He told them to get some salt and water and draw it up in a syringe. (Mickey just happened to have one in his pocket.) Jim did what Mickey said to do, but when Roy started throwing up, I fainted.

When I woke up, Roy was sitting up in the living room drinking a soda pop. I told Jay that I was ready to go, and Ms. Lynn said she was ready to go too. We put on our coats and got our things ready to go. Ms. Bertha gave us lots of food to take home, and we told everyone goodnight. Roy got up to leave with us, but Jay called him back into the kitchen, "Man, where do you think you're going?" Jay asked, looking angry and annoyed.

"I'm going home with you and Bee."

"No, Man, you don't have a home over there anymore." "But why, Jay?" Roy asked.

"Why? Cause you f–ed up tonight, My Man. You'll be staying here with Lenny."

"Hey, Man. I just made a mistake; I promise it won't happen again."

"Look, Roy, you made all of your mistakes in Miami. You don't get to make any here in Detroit with me."

"So it's like that, huh?" Roy backed away from Jay with a frown across his face.

"Yeah, Man, it's like that. I'll bring your things over tomorrow."

Ms. Lynn tried to talk to Jay. She begged him to give Roy another chance, but Jay told Ms. Lynn she knew Roy was wrong for doing what he did. If she didn't like it, she could stay there with her brother too.

"How could you treat your uncle so cold, Jay?" She cried to Jay.

"Bee, Roy is your problem. You need to find a way to help get him off of drugs. Find some type of program for him. I'll help you, if you want me to." Ms. Lynn went in the back to talk to Lenny. When she came back, she was ready to go. Lenny had refused to talk to Jay for her. He said that Roy needed some tough love, or he'd soon be locked up again.

CHAPTER 24

Roy's Drug Addiction

After that night, Roy would come over from time to time, sometimes to borrow money, sometimes to help out, and sometimes he'd even have a sob story. Ms. Lynn would give Roy money so he'd have clean clothes and decent shoes to wear. But he'd spend the money on drugs. If she bought clothes and gave them to him to stay clean, he'd sell the clothes and buy drugs.

Sometimes we'd give Roy money because he would try so hard to not have us mad at him, for reasons that he'd cause himself. Sometimes Roy would come over and clean up the house, take out the garbage, go to the store, and only ask for a pack of cigarettes. The last time Roy came over, we realized he had a motive for being so helpful. We had a few appliances missing. He'd set them out the back door while he was cleaning the kitchen and while we were watching TV. And when he went to the store for us, he took them away and sold them.

Our neighbor, Miss Jackson, saw everything that happened on our block. Ms. Jackson told us what Roy was doing. She'd seen him putting the things in a dirty, old box he had hidden on the side of the house. That was the same day I'd given Roy a ten-dollar bill to pick up pork chops for dinner for me. Roy sold our stuff and never came back with the pork chops.

After waiting four hours for him to come back, I realized that he'd done just what Jay told us he'd do. I was so upset because Jay also told us never to give Roy more than ten dollars, because it was just enough for him to buy enough drugs to overdose on. I was so nervous I couldn't sit down. All I could think about was Roy, somewhere dead from an overdose. What would Ms. Lynn say? What would she do to me? She's really going to hate me now, I thought.

Jay worked the second shift at the plant. I was waiting for him to come home so I could tell him what had happened. The minutes seemed like hours. I didn't know how he was going to react. It was twelve-thirty, and I heard Jay opening the door. When he looked at me, he knew something was wrong. He sat down beside me with a worried look on his face, "Hey, Babe, what's wrong?" he asked.

"I gave Roy ten dollars, and he never came back," I rambled on.

"Why did you give him ten dollars? He conned you just like I said he would, didn't he?" Jay's smile turned into laughter, and I was still rambling on.

"I sent him to the store to get some pork chops for dinner, and he never came back."

"Because he got you this time. He bought some drugs with the money. Why are you so upset, Louise?" Jay was still chuckling.

"Jay, don't laugh. You said that Roy might buy himself an overdose."

"Roy wishes he had enough money to buy that much dope so that he'd OD on it."

"I hope you're right, Jay," I said with relief in my voice.

"We won't see Roy for awhile. He's in our debt now. He knows what he's done, so he'll stay away from here for awhile."

CHAPTER 25

Three Weeks Later

It was almost Christmas, and no one had seen Roy, not even Diamond Jim. And he knew almost everything that was going down on the streets because his ladies of the night knew everything. And while Diamond Jim watched them, he knew everything they didn't tell him. He knew all of the hustlers, drug dealers, and con artists on the streets. He also knew where all of the junkies hung out, but no one had seen Roy.

Two days before Christmas, I was in the kitchen baking sweet potato pies when I heard someone banging on the door. It was Roy. I was glad to see him because he was not dead. Then I was mad at him for stealing the money, but mostly for having everyone worried.

"Hey, Sis, Merry Christmas. I have something for you." I could tell Roy had been doing drugs; his eyes were red, glassy, and almost closed when he smiled.

"Roy, is that all you have to say?"

"What do you want me to say, Sis, Ho-Ho-Ho?"

"What about my ten dollars you ran off with?" I snapped and closed the door, and put the chain on it.

"Come on, Sis, forget about the ten dollars. 'Tis the season to be jolly. Here, I have some gifts for you, let me in." Roy stood on the porch banging on the door.

"No, Roy, I won't let you in, not after what you did. Come back when Jay is home."

"You act as if I took a hundred dollars from you. What's the matter, your old man can't stand to give up ten dollars? All those punks at the plant make long bread, Sis. I'll bet Jay never shows you his pay check, and he never will. You need to let me in so I can s-c-h-o-o-l you, Girl." Roy started to laugh and I wanted to get rid of him.

"Good bye, Roy, I'll tell Jay you came by and what you had to say."

"You're going to tell Jay what I said? Don't be a fool, Girl. He'll always keep you in the dark." I had the security chain in place on the door, and I watched him as I talked to him. Roy was dirty. His clothes were two sizes too big, and his shoes were two sizes too small. His hands were so ashy; you'd have thought he had on white gloves. The gifts Roy had were dirty, and the wrapping paper was all wrinkled.

"Louise, you didn't let him in did you?" I knew Jay was mad by the look on his face.

"No, I made sure I talked to Roy with the chain securing the door."
"What did Roy have to say about the ten dollars?"

"Roy said to forget about the ten dollars. He said that you make long bread down at the plant, and that you could stand to give up ten dollars."

"What else did that clown have to say?"

Roy wanted me to let him in. "He said he had a lot of stuff to tell me about you."

"When I get my hands on that junky, he won't be able to try to start anymore trouble over here." I saw Ms. Lynn passing from her room to the kitchen. She'd heard me talking about Roy, and I knew she was going to get me. Jay was so mad that night; he went back out looking for Roy.

Jay came back three hours later, smelling like weed and booze. He walked past me, went into the room and fell across the bed. I was angry with Jay. I sat in the living room for awhile, because I didn't want to be near him. Ms. Lynn came in and told me that I talked too much, and that I should never have told Jay what had happened earlier that day, because he was under a lot of pressure. Then she said she didn't like trouble makers. And I told Ms. Lynn to stay out of my business.

I went back into our room and slammed the door. I just rolled Jay over to his side of the bed. I didn't even bother trying to help him take his clothes off. I just got myself dressed for bed and went to sleep.

On Christmas morning our neighbor, Miss Jackson, called Ms. Lynn to let her know that we had packages in front of our door. Jay went out to look, just in case it was something dangerous. Jay opened the door. "Look at this mess," he said, "I guess someone thinks this is funny." When I got to the door, there were the same packages Roy had brought by the day before, I felt really bad for Roy. It was Christmas Day, and he had no family to be with. I told Jay that those were the packages that Roy had with him when he came over on Christmas Eve. I told Jay how Roy had looked in his shabby clothes and too small shoes, and how he wasn't groomed at all. Ms. Lynn started to cry when I described her brother's appearance.

Jay said that he'd walk down the block to see if Roy was somewhere around, and that he could have Christmas with us. Jay went out looking for Roy. He came back two hours later, but no Roy. We looked for Roy for weeks, but we never heard from him. Jay said as long as we didn't hear from Roy, he must be doing alright. We all hoped Roy would be OK.

CHAPTER 26

Three Months Later

T he reality of being pregnant had finally set in. I had a small, little life growing inside of me, a helpless life depending on me. I thought about it all the time. It was time for my monthly check-up, and Jay drove me over to Dr Harper's office. After my check-up, I was still sitting in the exam room when Dr. Harper came back in and said that we should go into his office and sit down. Then he asked me how I felt about being a new mother. I said, "OK." Then Dr. Harper told me that I was going to be twice the mother I was before

—I was going to have twins. I felt faint, and nervous. I stood up and sat back down.

"But we don't want twins; we only want one," I begged Dr. Harper.

"Well, young lady, you're stuck with two." Dr. Harper saw how upset I was getting, and he sent the nurse to get Jay to come in.

"Louise, Babe, what's the matter?" he asked as he cuddled me. "Did they tell you?"

"Yeah, they told me, aren't you happy?" Jay said as he grinned as if we'd hit the jack pot or something.

"How can I be happy when I barely know how to take care of one baby? How am I going to take care of two? Your mother told me that childbirth could kill a person. If one baby doesn't kill me, then the other one will." I was so upset, I couldn't stop crying. The doctor had to give me something to calm me down.

After Jay heard how cruel Ms. Lynn had been to me, he assured me that I wouldn't die having our babies. The doctor said that I could get a spinal injection. It would keep me from being in such pain. At least it was an option. Jay and I agreed that an injection was the best choice. I just wanted to go home and sleep after all of the excitement.

Diamond Jim was having problems with his hookers, and Lenny had gotten really sick again—his diabetes had gotten out of control. Jay was left with taking full control of running The Club. Business was really good; he was raking it in. Jay even hired a host. He said that it would add elegance to The Club. Jay went part-time at the plant, so that he could run The Club. He had begun to love the night life that he'd been living, and I was upset most of the time.

I thought Ms. Lynn would like it that I was upset, because my friends were telling me that Jay had someone on the side. They said that it was Debbie, the Host that he'd hired. But I didn't believe them. Ms. Lynn was nice to me during those times. I even heard her tell Jay that he should call me more often, especially when he was out of the house two or three days at a time. Sometimes I'd be sleeping when Jay got in, and sleeping when he left.

In three weeks I'd be going into labor. I had already gone into false labor so many times that no one got excited anymore. Ms. Lynn had traumatized me with all the stories she'd told me about having a baby. She'd told me that the baby was going to rip my insides out, and here I was going to have two. I just knew I was going to die! During the time leading up to the big day, I sometimes wished that I could change my mind about having the babies. But there was no way that I could undo what I'd done. They had to come out. Ms. Lynn had told me there was only one way out, so I'd better prepare myself for a rude awakening.

CHAPTER 27

Having My Baby

On the night that I really went into labor, I kept going to the bathroom to pee. Ms. Lynn had noticed my frequent trips to the bathroom, and she came into my room and asked me how long had I been going like that. I told her every twenty minutes. As I was going back to my bed, I started wetting the floor. By the time I got back in the bed, the pains started coming again, every ten minutes. Ms. Lynn called the doctor and the hospital. When she called Jay, he said he'd be at the hospital as soon as someone came to relieve him. They'd hired a new guy to help Jay out; sometimes Troy would help out.

The nurse that admitted me took me in the back and prepped me. They told me to try to put my knees up to my chest as best as I could, while I was lying on my side. But every time the labor pains hit me, I'd flip onto my back and open my legs and scream. Ms. Lynn said that I should lie still as long as I could until I got the spinal, then the pains wouldn't hurt so badly. Even during my labor pains, I was still looking for Jay. Ms. Lynn had called The Club again, but Jay was not able to come to the hospital.

The labor pains were coming ten minutes apart, then five minutes apart. After the spinal, they had my legs strapped in some metal stirrups. The pain was getting greater, and I felt a lot of pressure. There was a room full of people looking right up my "couchie." All of my pride and dignity went right out of the window. After I felt the pressure, I got a light pain in my back. Then I felt something coming out; then I felt something else come out. I noticed everyone was rushing around very fast; they were really working. I could see the look on the doctor's face, and it didn't look like everything was OK. Then one of the nurses injected something into the tubing that they had going into my arm.

When I woke up again, the doctors were standing over me looking very concerned. They said that the 1st baby's weight was two pounds, and the 2nd baby's weight was one and a half pounds. He said that their lungs were very weak, and they were going to be on oxygen. If they lived past the first seventy- two hours, they'd be alright. I felt so alone and so helpless. I had no one there to support me.

I found out later that Ms. Lynn had gotten some bad news about Roy, and she had to get him out of Detroit. So she and the girls took him back to Miami. I still had not seen Jay. I cried for hours. They gave me another shot to calm me down. I went to sleep, and when I woke up again I remembered the bad news that I'd gotten about the babies.

I pushed the nurses' button and told the nurse that I was ready to see the babies. She said that I had to eat and have my meds, and then she'd take me. While I was waiting, I thought about who the babies looked like. Were they looking for me? Would they know that I was their mother when they saw me? I had a million and one things running through my head. But I could hardly wait to see the little strangers.

The nurse came in the room to get me. "It's time to see your twins; I'm going to walk over there with you," she said.

"Thanks, I need some company." "You look scared," she said.

"I am scared," I said as I tied the belt to the silk robe that Jay had bought me for the occasion. It made me think about him, and it made me sad because he wasn't there. "The doctor said that the babies were very sick, so I have to at least show up and let them know I'm here for them, right?" I said to the nurse, hoping that she'd tell me things had changed for the better since I'd talked to the doctor.

"Well, we're doing everything that we can. Where is their father?" The nurse asked with concern.

"I don't know," I answered. I knew by the way she looked at me, that I meant the father hadn't been around for awhile. But I didn't care, my babies were my concern then, and nothing else mattered. I had always thought that Jay would be there with me when I went into labor. Instead, the babies were sick, and I had to do all of the worrying and crying alone. The nurse and I talked as we walked down a long hall that seemed like a mile. We finally got to the nursery window, and I saw the twins for the first time. I wanted to cry; they didn't look good at all. I thought they were going to die at any moment; they were so frail and lifeless. If I could hold one of them, she'd fit into one of my hands. And her head was no bigger than a medium-size orange.

I stood at that nursery window and cried until my legs were weak. On my way back to my room, I noticed something warm running down my legs. I looked down, and it was blood. I'd been standing too long. I grabbed the hand-rail along the wall, and everything went black. When I woke up, it was the next day.

As soon as I had my breakfast, I went down the hall to the nursery again. When I got there, I saw only one baby; one of my babies was not there! I banged on the window to get the nurse's attention. Then I cried out, as loud as I could, so she'd turn around, "Where is my baby?" The nurse pointed to Baby A. I could see her dialing the phone, and I was trying to get in the door to where she was. "I had two babies, and you know it," I screamed. I felt someone behind me, pulling me down into a wheelchair, and then a stick in my arm.

When I woke up again, the Doctor was standing beside my bed, holding a light to my eyes. He later told me that Baby B had died of multiple complications. I felt so bad for my little girl; I never even got a chance to hold her or even touch her. She never felt the caress of my hands, and yet she was gone from my sight, gone forever. I cried for her. I cried for myself. And I cried because Jay never got to see her alive.

My world as I knew it had been turned up-side-down, and I didn't even have a shoulder to cry on. I'd left the only family that cared anything about me back in Miami, I thought. It was a long way home, but that's where I needed to be. I was a new mother trying to deal with the sickness of my baby girl, and the death of her twin sister. Even though I never held my baby, in my heart I felt that she was still alive. I wanted to see her, but the nurse said, "Later." I didn't believe that my baby was really dead.

A woman came into my room that evening. She said that I was doing fine, and that I would be discharged the next day. She said that my baby would have to stay in the hospital for six weeks, or until she was at least six pounds. I asked to see the baby that they told me had died. I needed to touch her, just hold her in my arms. I needed some closure, but the nurse didn't seem to be sensitive to my loss at all. She acted as though there never had been another baby. I didn't even have a chance to grieve over my child.

That nurse was cold. She just wanted me to know that I had to leave the next day. I wanted to see someone else regarding my baby. They sent someone in, and she told me that the whole ordeal was too over-whelming for me, and that I should wait a few days, and whatever I wanted would be alright. I didn't understand how they were handling things, but what did I know? It was all new to me, and I had no one to tell me what I should do about the situation.

I kept thinking, if only Jay was there, he'd know what to do about our baby. And then I thought that maybe he'd done what his mother wanted him to do, leave me with a baby. I couldn't sleep that night. I kept on thinking. What is happening to me? Am I asleep and can't wake-up?

CHAPTER 28

Back in Love Again

The next day I took a taxi back to our apartment. When I got upstairs, I put the key in the lock, and someone opened the door. I looked up, and it was Jay, standing there looking stupid. His eyes were red, his clothes smelled like weed, and his breath smelled like he'd not brushed his teeth for days. He even had stains all over his shirt. I'd never seen Jay looking like that. He was always groomed and well-kept. "What's wrong with you, why are you looking like that?" I wanted to know.

"I called the hospital, and they said you'd been discharged already. I was going to bring you home today. Where are the twins? Why didn't you bring them home too?" Jay looked pitiful. He was looking out of the window and out the door for the babies.

"Jay, stop it. The babies are not here. One of them is still at the hospital, and the other one is dead." He stood still for a few minuets; he didn't even breathe. Then he walked over to the couch and sat next to me.

"Dead! What do you mean one of them is dead? And why is the other one still in the hospital?" Jay grabbed both of my shoulders and was squeezing them; I pushed him away from me.

"Damn you Jay, if you had thought about us even one day, you'd know what happened. They wouldn't let me see the one that died. They act as if I just lost a shoe or something. I needed you, and you weren't there. I had no one to help me fight for my babies, no one!"

I went into our bedroom to get away from Jay. I slammed the door, lay across the bed, and closed my eyes. I could hear Jay outside the door trying to explain why he never made it to the hospital. After Jay explained everything, the bottom line was, The Club and his uncle's affairs were more important than his family. And his solution to his problems was to get high and drunk, and it would all go away. At least that's the way I looked at it.

"Louise, please believe me. I wanted to be there with you. I couldn't just leave the place in Troy's hands; he's not that reliable."

"Jay, when it comes to your family, you're not that reliable. So go to the hospital if you're really that concerned. Find out what happened to your daughter for yourself. And when, and if, you come back, I won't be here."

"What do you mean by that, you won't be here?"

"Just go, Jay. Get the hell out of my face." He got in the car and went to the hospital.

When Jay got to the hospital, he was in a rage, and the Hennessey was all over his breath. The receptionist at the front desk called for security. If Jay had not been in the shape he was in, he could have handled the matter in a better way. Instead, he was escorted out of the hospital and warned not to come back like that.

I hated Jay, and I didn't want to hear his reasons for not visiting me and the babies at the hospital. I didn't want to see his face ever again. I finally got up enough nerve to call Mama. After I told Mama that I wanted to stay in Detroit with Jay, I hadn't wanted to call her again for any reason. But now I had to think about my baby girl.

I needed Mama to tell me what I should do about my baby that had died. I needed Mama to tell me how to stop hurting. I needed my mama. I needed Mama to comfort me, to tell me everything was going to be alright. After I talked to Mama, I felt a lot better. I just needed to hear her voice.

She told me to have Jay go back to the hospital with me to find out what had happened, and if I still wanted to come home when the baby was able to leave the hospital, she'd send for both of us. Mama said she wanted me to call her collect every week to let her know how I was doing.

When I hung up the phone, I had to find a place to stay for the next six weeks. When the baby was discharged, we were going back to Miami, but I needed a place to live until then. As I sat on the edge of the bed, I could see Mrs. Jackson on her porch, and I thought of how she and Mama had taken to each other. They had talked all the time when Mama was visiting us. She'd told Mama that if I ever needed help, I could always go to her.

I went next door and told Mrs. Jackson what the situation was. She agreed to let me stay there, if I agreed to at least sit down and talk to Jay before I left for Florida. We agreed that I didn't have to do it that night, but I would soon. I asked Mrs. Jackson not to say anything about me staying with her to Jay until I was ready. She said, OK. Mrs. Jackson said that Jay needed to see how it felt to not know where I was, like I did when he didn't show up at the hospital.

I went back to the apartment and packed as fast as I could. I took my things over to Mrs. Jackson's, and she took me to my room. From my window, I could see the street and everything that moved on it, all the way down the block. I unpacked my things and went back to the window to see if Jay had returned yet.

As soon as I pulled the curtain back, I saw him and his Uncle Lenny getting out of the car. Lenny was moving kind of slow. I thought that maybe his sickness had gotten worse. Jay hurried to get to the apartment building. I ran into the kitchen and told Mrs. Jackson that Jay had gotten back. She told me to stay in my room and out of the way. She said she'd answer the door if he came over. Sure enough the door bell rang, and it was Jay. Mrs. Jackson said that he looked scared and almost in tears.

"Mrs. Jackson, have you seen my wife?"

"You don't know where your wife is?" Ms. Jackson asked as she looked at Jay over her glasses.

"Please, Mrs. Jackson, did you see anyone come to pick her up?" Mrs. Jackson stood in the door way and just watched Jay as he nervously looked back at our apartment and continued to question her, "Was she walking? Was anyone with her? Did you see anything?"

"No, Jay, but I'll keep an eye out for her. You want to leave a message in case I do?"

"Please tell Louise to call me and give her this. I know she doesn't have any money because she left it in the drawer. Tell her that I love her, and I'm sorry." Jay gave Mrs. Jackson $300.00 to give to me.

"OK, I'll do that," Ms. Jackson answered.

Jay walked back to the car with his head down, looking sad. Lenny was behind him, walking even slower. With his swollen feet, he could hardly keep up with Jay. (I'd always told Lenny that Bertha was going to kill him with her good cooking and baking that he loved so much.) When they drove off, I thought about what Mama had said about going back home. Then I wished that I'd finished the nursing program so that when I did go back home, I'd have a job I'd be proud of. I didn't want to just show up with a baby and no way of supporting her.

Three weeks passed, and I was taking a bus every other day to the hospital to see my baby girl. She was the only reason I was staying alive. She was looking reached six pounds yet, I was still able to hold her and let her know that I was her mother.

Jay had been visiting Mrs. Jackson's home every week to see if I'd been by there. One day when he came, Mrs. Jackson told Jay that she'd seen me, given me the money, and told me what Jay had said. When she told me what she'd done, she reminded me of the talk I needed to have with Jay about our situation. I promised Mrs. Jackson that I'd have that talk.

The next week I was sitting at the bus stop waiting for the bus to come, and Jay drove up and insisted that I get into the car, and I did. I thought I may as well get it over with. Jay drove to the apartment. It was really hot that day. When we got inside, I went to the fridge and got a cold drink. I really wanted to take a shower to cool off, but I didn't want Jay to get any ideas, or even think that we were back together. My plan was that I'd hear what he had to say, and then I'd let him know that the baby and I were going to Miami.

But Jay had other plans. He tried to set the mood. He played the Temptations singing "Since I Lost My Baby" while we talked. I'd heard that song a thousand times. Every time Jay would go to Mrs. Jackson's door and she said that she'd not seen me, he'd go back to the apartment and play that song over and over again. And when he'd leave to go back to The Club or back to Lenny's house, on the way to his car, the kid that played on the block would sing that song to him as he got into the car.

Jay sat down beside me and tried to explain to me again why he hadn't been at the hospital. He said the first night he couldn't get anyone to relieve him, so he was going to visit the next day. The second night, he had a few drinks with the boys to celebrate our twins birth. He'd worked so late the night before that he had overslept. When he woke up, it was too late to visit.

"Jay, why didn't you just call me?"

"Every time I'd call, they said that you were out of the room."
"Did you even ask about the babies?"

"I did, and she said it was against hospital policies to give out any information. And I asked about you every time I called." I couldn't believe that the nurse never told me anything.

"Louise, please tell me what happened."

I explained to Jay that the babies were so small that their lungs were not fully developed. They'd given them seventy-two hours to survive, and if they made it, they would be strong enough to fight. I told Jay the smaller baby had died, and how insensitive they were. They never even let me see her. Jay started to cry, and so did I. We comforted each other. I stayed all night, and we made love.

CHAPTER 29

Only the Strong Survive

The next morning we drove to the hospital. We went to the nursery first, so that Jay could see our new, baby girl. The nurse came out, and we told her who we were. She helped us gown-up, and we went over to our daughter's bed. I told Jay to sit down, and I picked the baby up and gave her to Jay. She was still so small, he was afraid to hold her, but he did. Everyone in the nursery knew me because I'd come so often.

While Jay held the baby, I talked to the nurses to see how she was doing. They told me that she'd be able to go home that day, and I told Jay the news. We were very happy, but we still had a situation to take care of regarding our other twin daughter. I told them to have Vanessa ready when got back, so that we could take her home.

Jay and I went to the Administrator's Office, and I told them what had happened, as much as I could remember. They laid everything on me at one time. First my baby was dead. Then I had to leave the next day without my other baby. Then they told me that I couldn't see the baby that they said had died. They told me not to worry about her, and it was too soon for me to see my baby anyway. I started to cry again.

They asked me if I had signed any papers acknowledging that I was told that my baby had expired. I said, No. One of the administrators asked how could they know what had happened, if I didn't even know what the doctor had told me about the baby's death. I didn't know. I felt like a fool. I'd trusted them all, and now they were acting like there never was another baby.

Jay blew-up and went off on all of them. They called security, and four officers came into the office. Jay told them each to back off and to get out of our way, and that we were going to the nursery to get our baby. Jay also told them that we were going to sue them. We left their office and went to the nursery, but security followed us there and out the door. I cried all the way home. Everytime I looked at Vanessa, I thought about her twin. I couldn't believe that my other baby was dead. I didn't feel it in my heart, maybe it was because I needed some closure.

When we got to the apartment Mrs. Jackson was on her porch; she waved and we waved back. When she saw the baby, she came over. She held Vanessa and told Jay to get his affairs in order, because I was going to need all the help I could get with the baby. I soon learned that being grown-up was harder than I'd imagined. It meant making the right decisions and being responsible for the decisions that you do make, and the things that you do. I'd learned a lot, but I still had a lot to learn. I was getting a taste of the real world.

A month passed, and I still had not called Mama back, even though she told me to come on back home. Jay and I had made up, and anytime I considered staying with Jay or going back home, Jay would win every time. I was addicted to Jay, and I couldn't shake him. Jay had gone back to work full-time at the plant. He'd go in and work a few nights a week at The Club, as we needed the money.

Lenny had sent for one of his brothers that had returned from Viet Nam to help run The Club. That was a bad idea. I knew the very first night I met Dennis that he'd be a bad influence on Jay. He was also bad news for anyone he came in contact with. That guy was crazy. All he ever talked about was Viet Nam or the Viet Cong. He talked about what happened over there constantly, bloody bodies and guns. Sometimes Jay had to make him stop because Dennis's conversation gave Jay flashbacks from Viet Nam, and they gave me nightmares from all the bloody stories.

By the end of the summer, they closed The Club down and sold it for less than they wanted to. Lenny's illness was getting worse, and Diamond Jim couldn't control his hookers or his drug habit. He was going down, and no one took Diamond Jim seriously anymore. They also sent Dennis, the deranged demon, back to Florida. I was happy that Jay was coming home every night after he left the plant.

But I was always worried about him because they were having trouble over in Philadelphia and Chicago. Young black brothers were being harassed by the police. They were forced to stop and get out of their cars for no reason. We started having some trouble in Detroit too. Jay had always said that he'd go to jail or hell before he'd let them disrespect him.

I always waited up for Jay; I couldn't sleep until I saw him. In December of that year, Mark Clark and Fred Hampton, leaders of the Black Panther Party in Chicago, were killed. Police broke through the doors of their house and fired rounds of ammunition at them. I was saddened and very upset about that terrible event. Because of their insistence on defending themselves, they had become targets of the police and/or the FBI.

One week had passed since I'd heard that awful news about the Panthers, and then Jay came in looking like he'd been fighting. I flew off of the couch and hurried to the door. When I saw him, I asked, "Jay, what happened to you?"

"Don't worry, Babe, it wasn't the police. I know you worry about me."

"Who were you fighting then?" Jay's nose was bleeding, his fists were skinned up, his always neatly-combed afro was messed up and had dirt in it, and the collar of his leather coat was torn and hanging on by a thread.

"We're on strike at Fleetwood, and they want to bring in other workers.

When they crossed the picket line, we all got into a fight."

"Are you going back tomorrow?" "Yes, Babe, I have to."

"Why?" I cried as I helped Jay take off his ragged, leather coat.

"Don't you worry about that, I have some good news for you. I'm sending you and Vanessa to Miami next week. You'll be home in time for Christmas."

"Look, Jay, I'm not the little girl that I was when you met me. Don't tell me you have good news for me, and just send me back home for awhile, with everything going on around here. Tell me something else."

"OK, Louise, I don't know what's going to happen with this job. We may have to move back to Florida for good. Things may get worse at the plant, and I want to know that my family is safe. Please don't fight me on this."

"Where will we live, Jay?" I asked as I looked around the room, because life as I knew it would never be the same, once I went back home. I knew Mama loved me, but I'd be her little girl again.

"Call your mom or mine and tell them that we need a place to stay. I'll pay them rent until we find a place of our own." It was late, but I called Mama anyway. When the phone rang, Bobbie answered the phone.

"Hello."

"Hi, who is this?"

"It's Bobbie. What's happened? You're calling so late."

"Nothing, everything is alright. Where is Mama? I just wanted to let you all know that I'm coming home for Christmas."

"Mama's sleeping, Louise. But I'm glad you called, because I was going to call you. I'm getting married on Christmas Eve, and I want you to be my maid of honor."

"Yes, Bobbie, I'd love to. But the last time I talked to Mama, she said that your boyfriend was in Viet Nam."

"He's not my boyfriend anymore. I had to write him a Dear Jim letter in October."

"Why, what happened?"

"You know that girl Lorie that lives around the corner? She went to school with you."

"OK, what about her?" "Well, she had his baby." "How do you know?"

"It's a long story. When you come home, I'll tell you the rest of that story and who I'm going to marry. I'll tell Mama you called. Love ya."

"Love ya back."

I hadn't realized how long I'd been sitting out front thinking about my life up to this point. So much had happened since the last time I sat on this porch. But now it's time to get up from these porch steps and leave those memories, I thought. Time to go into the house and face Daddy and Mama. I'd been gone a long time, a long way from home, but this was where I needed to be for now.

CHAPTER 30

No Place Like Home

Bobbie and Freddy were married on Christmas Eve. I was her Maid of Honor, and I was also five months pregnant. It was a beautiful, winter wedding; she had four bride's maids, two flower girls and a ring bearer. Her colors were burgundy and white. Bobbie and Freddy were a match made in heaven, and the two of them couldn't have been happier. They moved into a small apartment on Biscayne Blvd.

I spent the first two weeks that I was back home, helping Bobbie with her wedding. When she got back from her two-day honeymoon, Freddy went to work, and we spent time together getting caught up on each other's lives. When she returned to work, I knew that she'd want time with her husband, and I could see what was going on with my girls, Sandy and Joy.

I decided to call Sandy and let her know that I was back in town. "Hello, may I speak to Sandy?"

"Sandy doesn't live here anymore! Who is this?"

"It's Louise. I'm back in Miami, and I just thought I'd let her know I'm back."

"Louise, Sandy got married and moved out about eight months ago."

"Do you have a number for her?" Sandy's mom gave me her phone number, and I wrote it down and hung up the phone. I wondered if Sandy married Sid.

Or did she break up Ben's family and marry him? I dialed Sandy's number. The phone rang, but no answer. Then I decided to give Joy a call. I hadn't talked to her since I went into the hospital to have my babies. She probably didn't even know about Vanessa's twin. I dialed Joy's number, and someone picked up.

"Hello."

"Hi, is Joy at home?"

"No! I haven't seen Joy in two days; she hangs out with that crook all the time now, and anyway, who is this?"

"Nobody."

I hung up the phone. Fine time to ask who it was, after he'd put her business out, I thought. Joy's father always had seemed a little shaky to me. He never seemed to be dealing with a full deck. In other words, I thought he was nuts. I couldn't wait to talk to Joy, to see what kind of crook her father thought she was hanging out with.

I called back three hours later. Joy was home, and she wanted to talk. I told her about the twins and everything that had happened. We talked about Ms. Lynn, Roy, her sister Sue, and her brother Gene, and what they've been doing. And then we talked about Joy. And from our conversation I could tell that Joy had no intentions of graduating from high school. She was looking for some man to take care of her, and she always caught up with someone else's man. Sometimes she'd tread the waters by dating someone unattached. Then she'd leave one relationship one day and explore another the next. Joy was just out of control. She gave me a number where she could be reached. She said that she had some things that she needed to take care of, and that her boyfriend would bring her over to see Vanessa later. I hung up, and went in to see what Mama was doing.

Mama was home, and she was about to sweep all of the nap off of the rug. Mama hadn't changed. I could always tell when something was wrong with Mama—she couldn't stop sweeping. She'd sweep some more trash into the dust pan and look at me. She asked, "How is the baby?"

I'd say, "Fine," and then I'd ask her, "Mama, what's wrong?"

"It's your sister, Anne. She and Al have been having really nasty fights." "Fights about what, Mama?"

"They fight because he's drinking too much. Al's a good man from Monday through Friday, but when he starts to drink, he gets crazy."

"So why doesn't Anne just tell him to leave?"

"She can't, Louise. She can't leave those kids without a father, it just ain't right." I was so mad with Mama for saying it was OK for Al to fight my sister.

"Mama, why are you taking up for Al when he's hitting on your daughter?

And what is Daddy saying, does he approve of this?"

"Well, Al is a good man, he makes good money, and he always takes good care of Anne and those kids. Sometimes it's not so bad."

I told Mama that I thought Anne's marriage was headed for divorce. Mama got very up-set and told me to forget she ever said anything if I had to say a terrible thing like that about Anne's marriage. Mama had a thing about commitment. Once you were with a man, that was it. You should stay with him no matter what. Maybe that's why I'd let Jay get away with so much, I'd been brainwashed. Although Jay never hit me, or ever said a harsh word to me, it was just the things he'd done.

Anyway, Mama started to sweep again, and I heard Vanessa crying. I went into the room and picked her up. Mama came in and said that I should let the baby cry more. She said that every time Vanessa cried,

I ran in and snatched her. Mama said that Vanessa's lungs needed to get stronger, because now she sounded like a sick cat when she cried. Mama was right. When Vanessa was born, both babies had weak lungs. But how did she know? I never told Mama about what the doctor had said about Vanessa's lungs, but Mama seemed to know everything. She even knew that I was pregnant before I told her. I brought the baby into the living room and gave her to Mama. I got a bottle ready for Vanessa in the kitchen and gave it to Mama. We sat and watched two of her soaps.

The doorbell rang. I opened the door, and it was Joy. I gave her a big hug and let her in, but as I closed the door, a big, very well-dressed man pushed the door open and stepped inside. Joy introduced us. And I thought this must be the crook Joy's father was talking about.

"Louise, this is Sam." "Hi Sam."

"Sam, this is my sister in-law, Louise." Joy gave me an address where she wanted to get together later—at Sam's place. She kissed the baby, and I opened the door for them. As they left, I noticed that Joy had lost at least twenty pounds, and her once, sixteen-year-old-looking face looked at least thirty-five. She noticed that I was studying her face, and she turned her head and talked to me as she looked out of the window.

"OK, Louise, call me if you need a ride, and we'll pick you up."

"OK, Sis, thanks for coming over, and nice meeting you, Sam." Sam seemed to be in a hurry, and Mama was looking at Joy and shaking her head.

"What happened to that girl, Louise? She used to be a pretty child when she used to come over, and now she's beginning to look like one of those street women."

"I don't know, Mama. I guess she just needs to slow down."

"That's a full-grown man that child is running around with. She's going to run into trouble with that one. Mark my word." I never liked it when Mama said, "Mark my word," because you were doomed.

The phone rang. I picked it up; it was Sandy.

"Hi Girly, this is Sandy, when did you get back in town?"

"Just recently." I didn't even want to get into why I've been home for two weeks and haven't contacted her.

"We thought you'd never come back to Miami this soon; how's married life?" "It's OK. Your mom told me that you had gotten married too."

"Yeah," she laughed.

"Why are you laughing? Who did you marry?"

"I married, Sid." Sandy didn't sound too excited. She gave me her address and asked if I could come over to talk.

CHAPTER 31

Closure

I finally got a chance to visit Sandy's apartment; it was a duplex. The outside was very well kept, and I saw that she had a little, green Volkswagen that had a gold-plated tag on the front that said "SANDY." I gathered Vanessa's things and took her out of the car. I knocked on the door with one hand and rocked Vanessa with the other arm. Finally, she opened the door and said, "Hey girl, I see you had to bring your baby."

"Yeah, I did ask Mama to keep Vanessa until I got back, but Mama said that I was the one who had a good time getting her, so I should take her with me." We laughed, and I followed Sandy into her room. I laid Vanessa down on the bed and covered her. She slept for a while. Sandy had the A/C on, and it was nice and quite in her room.

When I walked back into the living room, Sandy has made drinks for both of us, Long Island Ice Teas. She took a pack of Kools from her purse, and we started to laugh because both of us thought about the Island Club. We talked about the fun we'd had before I left. Then I noticed that Sandy's eyes stayed glued on her front, living room window. "Sandy are you expecting someone?"

"I'm looking to see if Ben is still driving by to check on me." "Sandy, do you mean Ben comes by your house?"

"Yeah, Girl, we're still tipping around." Sandy acted as if it was OK to tip around after she was married.

"Why did you marry Sid, if you're still seeing Ben?" "Ben and I have a love /hate thing going on." "Well, why don't you tell me about it?"

"After graduation, I got a job with Southern Bell Phone Company. I was still having an affair with Ben while seeing Sid. Ben wanted to leave his wife and live with me, but I couldn't control Ben like I can Sid, and if Ben had left his wife, he'd expect too much from me. So, I refused his offer. But I was having fights with my dad, because every time I'd go out with Ben, I was getting in too late. I needed to move. Then Sid found out about Ben, and he figured if we got married, Ben wouldn't be a problem anymore. I couldn't afford to move out on my own, so I married Sid. He was a way out. I even told Sid that I wasn't really in love with him when he asked me to marry him. But he said that he wanted to get married anyway."

We heard a car drive by again, and Sandy got up and stood by her front window. She sipped more of her drink and smiled.

"What's going on Sandy?"

"Oh it's nothing, that's just Ben. He sees your car parked out front, and he doesn't know who is visiting me, and he's going crazy."

"Well Sandy, I hope things work out for you. I just feel sorry for Sid. He's always loved you, but that's not my problem. Anyway, I'm leaving."

"Yeah, that would be the best thing for you to do; I don't need your judgmental attitude around me today."

I went in and got Vanessa and her diaper bag and headed out the door. I didn't want to fight with Sandy. I just said, "Bye." I walked out the door, went to the car and laid the baby on the seat. (Mama had let me use her little put-put to visit Sandy.) As I walked around to the other side, I heard a car driving toward me. I looked up, and it was

Ben driving by. I waved good bye to Sandy and got in the car. I could see Ben parked on the corner. I backed out and drove in the other direction because I didn't even want to look at him.

When I returned to Mama's, I went into my room to lay the baby down, and the mail man had come while I was out. There was mail on my bed—a letter from Jay telling me that Fleetwood, the plant where he worked, has completely closed down, and that he'd be returning to Miami soon. That was great news, and I felt like celebrating, but I got a wave of morning sickness. I sat on the bed and rubbed my belly. Mama said that it helped to get rid of that sick feeling, and it did. Mama had delivered enough babies to know all the tricks of the trade.

When Jay came, it was going to feel funny sleeping in the same bed with him, I thought, especially with Mama right down the hall. Things really had changed around there. Sometimes when we all sat watching TV, and I was feeding Vanessa, they watched us as though we were strangers. I never would be the same to them again, but everything changes, nothing stays the same.

Jay and his uncle drove down from Detroit in two days. I had missed Jay so much, and I was excited to see him. I knew Vanessa would be glad to see her father too. I walked out on the porch, and I saw Bobbie pull up in the new car her husband had bought for her. Freddy was always doing nice things for Bobbie. I was glad that she came over so we could talk some more.

It felt good being around family again. Anne and her kids had come over the night before, and she had told Mama that she and Al were through. Anne said that she told Al to pack his bags and leave. She said the fighting had to stop before someone was killed. The fighting was getting too violent. They had three kids then, and Al loved them all, but he loved the alcohol just as much. Anne said that divorce was the only answer.

Anne was sending her husband away, but with good reason. And I was waiting for mine to return. Jay had called the day before to say that they were still on the road and would be coming into Miami in the morning. I could hardly wait. I only wished that he was flying in. I didn't like Jay traveling with Jim; he was no good for Jay.

Ten o'clock the next morning I was sitting on the front porch with Vanessa. A car pulled up, and it was Jay and his uncle. I got up and opened the screen door, and Jay was getting out of the car as fast as he could. I hurried out to meet him with Vanessa on my hip, and when we met Jay took Vanessa, hugged and kissed her and then me. I could taste the Hennessey he'd been drinking on his breath. I pushed his face away; I didn't like it, but I was glad to see him, so I let it go. Jim had been using drugs again, and he couldn't even get out of the car yet. Daddy and the rest of the family were standing on the porch watching us. Jay gave Vanessa back to me and went up to greet them. Mama told Jay that she was going to fix all of his favorite foods for dinner that night; he thanked her and gave her a hug. Jay shook Daddy's hand and went back to help Jim out of the car.

Jay only got some of his things out of the car and put them in our room, and I went in behind him. Jay closed the door and told me that we'd have to go back to Detroit. He said that he'd found an attorney, and that we were going back to see about our twin, baby daughter. Jim had some business to take care of in Miami. Jay had already bought our plane tickets, and he said that I should pack something for two days, and that we'd let the family know our plans at dinner. When I heard the news, I cried tears of joy; it gave me hope that I'd see my baby girl. I prepared a garment bag for us, and I even packed some of Vanessa's new things. If we brought her twin back with us, she'd look nice.

We had dinner, and Jay and I told the family of our tragedy with the twins, and what we planned to do about it. Mama said that she'd keep Vanessa for me while we were gone. We were to leave at 8 AM the next morning. Jay and his uncle went out for awhile, and while they were gone, all I could think about was bringing my baby back with me. I didn't feel like eating any dinner, and I knew that I wouldn't be able to sleep. I just felt that somehow my baby was still alive, and I wanted to see her.

At 7 AM Jay and I got ready to go to the airport. I changed Vanessa and gave her a bottle. Then I picked her up and took her to Mama's room and put her in between her and Daddy. They smiled, and Daddy wished me good luck, and said that he hoped everything turned out alright for us. Jim took us to the airport.

I cried all the way to the airport. Jim said that I was making him nervous, and Jay tried to comfort me. Jay and I only had the one garment bag to check in when we got to the airport. I kept the clothes for the baby in a diaper bag with me. We boarded the plane, and I clutched my baby's diaper bag all the way to Detroit. We arrived in Detroit, got our bag, and Jay called a taxi. We got in, and he drove us up town, right to the State Attorney's office. We got on the elevator, and I got sick again.

When we walked into the office where our case was being held, everyone was looking at me like I'd lost my mind. I held onto my baby's diaper bag and looked around the room for her. I didn't know what to expect at that meeting, but I did expect to see my baby. However, I didn't see her—she was nowhere in sight. We all sat down, and everyone in the room watched me clutch the diaper bag that I'd brought in with me.

A lady got up and read a report of some sort. After she finished her report, I started to cry and I couldn't control my tears. I hugged the diaper bag as tight as my arms would let me. I started feeling sick again. Jay tried to comfort me, as he reminded me that getting upset was not good for the pregnancy. He'd known about the fate of our baby all along, and he'd never told me.

During the report I learned that after my baby had died, she was so small that they didn't want to take her to the morgue right away. They had put her in a backroom on a table so that she could be wrapped properly. Someone had come along and thought she was a misplaced

1 ½ lb. fetus, and she had been sent to their medical school of biology within the hospital and preserved as an infant specimen. The Labor and Delivery Department had lost my baby and tried to cover it up. They'd realized that I was a young girl with no family support and that I had no knowledge of procedures in a situation like that.

After the attorney that Jay had hired investigated the hospital and medical records, they found two birth certificates. One of them had Vanessa as a single birth, and the other one was for twins, and one had expired. We were awarded

$70,000. But after Jay paid back all the cash advances he'd borrowed, and by the time we finished paying the attorney's fee, we returned to Miami with $20,000 and a broken heart.

We took a taxi into the city, and the taxi stopped in front of a funeral home where Jay had our baby daughter put into a casket. It was there sitting in the chapel. At least I had peace of mind knowing for sure that she wasn't alive. I wanted to remember her as the tiny little baby I had seen in the nursery, and not as a specimen. I said good bye to her, and at that point I finally had some closure with my baby's death. I wanted to return to Miami right away, but our flight didn't leave until the next day.

We got back into the taxi and went to Lenny's house. When we went inside, everyone wanted to know what had happened. Jay told them about the report and what the investigative attorney had found and that he had a victory in the court room that day. But all I saw was defeat. My baby girl was gone from my sight forever. I didn't want to stop and talk to anyone. I let Jay entertain them. I went to the room to lie down and tried to sleep until it was time for us to leave the next day.

We boarded the plane at 6 AM the next day, and I was still numb. Jay held my hand and told me to try and stay calm. I wondered how long I'd hurt like that, how long my insides would feel like they'd been ripped out. I guessed that the emptiness, the pain, and the hurt would be with me for a long time.

CHAPTER 32

Robert or Lil Jay

At 10:31 AM, we arrived at Miami International Airport. We went to baggage claim and picked up our one garment bag, and Jay flagged down a taxi to take us home. My heart ached because I wasn't bringing my baby home. I started to cry again. When we got to the house, Jay told Daddy what had happened. Mama looked at me, and she could see that I'd been crying. She also saw that I was still clutching the diaper bag that I had taken with me. As I walked to my room, I could hear Mama following me. I sat on the bed still holding onto the diaper bag, and I stared into space while Mama sat down beside me.

She said to me, "Baby, I can tell you from experience, I know what it feels like to loose a child. I lost three sons. Two still births, and one died two days after he was born. I know just how deep it hurts, and so does God. When the pain is too hard to bear, call on His name. You can always tell Him about your pain, and He'll ease it for you. So hold your head up and be a woman because you still have Vanessa to take care of and another child on the way to think about." She was right. I leaned over on Mama, and I wet her chest with my tears. Mama rubbed my shoulders and said, "It's OK, Baby. You cry if you have to, just get it all out."

I stopped crying, and I said, "Mama, I'm so sorry I left home and caused you to have high blood pressure. Now I know what it feels like when your child is gone from your sight and you don't know what to do." I think Mama and I were best friends from then on.

I heard Vanessa crying, and I jumped up from the bed to see what was wrong with her, but I thought about what Mama had said about her lungs not being strong. I stopped and looked at Mama, and she said, "Girl, go on in there and get that Howlin' Jack." I laughed and I thought, Mama has given Vanessa a nickname already. I didn't hear her crying anymore, so I walked into the living room, and Jay had picked her up and was playing with her.

The doorbell rang, and I answered it. I opened the door, and it was Jim. He seemed to be in a hurry, and he wanted to talk to Jay. They talked, and Jay told me that he needed to go with Jim to take care of some business. He said that he'd be right back, and they left. At 12 AM Jay still wasn't back. I was thinking that my parents must think that my husband was a jerk, because I did. What was he doing?

9 AM the next morning, Jay knocked on my bedroom window and told me to open the door. I hurried to the front door and let Jay in. We walked back to our room and closed the door. We sat on the bed. "Listen, Louise," he said, "I need to go back to Detroit with Jim, and we need to leave today."

"Jay! What is going on? What in the hell are you and Jim doing? And what kind of business are you taking care of?"

"Babe, I promise when I get back, I'll sit down and tell you everything. Please don't be mad at me."

"Jay, please don't go with Jim, because if you do, the next time you see me things won't be the same between us."

"Louise, please try to understand what I'm trying to do. I'm doing this for you, for us, for our family."

"Well, you need to let me know what's going on, right now."

"Babe, the less you know, the better off you are. I love you." Jay gave me a peck on the cheek, threw some things in his traveling bag, and left.

Three months later Jay was still in Detroit. He had called and written letters. He'd even sent money for me to get an apartment and to shop for new furniture. He'd also called Daddy and asked him if he'd go with me to shop for a car, if I wanted to get one before he got back. Every week I looked to hear from Jay by telegraph or telephone, but at the end of our conversation, or his letters, one would bring bad news, and the other one would give me the blues, because he never would say when he was coming home.

It was May, and I was due to deliver the baby any day. Jay had called me almost every day saying that the baby was making him sick. He said that he was even having labor pains, and that he was suffering with me. I just wanted to slap him every time he said that. Sometimes I even hung up the phone when I heard his voice. Mama said that the baby was going to look just like Jay, because I was mad at him all the time.

One morning Jay called me and said that he'd be home in two days. I wondered if he'd get there before I had the baby. May 9th at 11:30 PM, I couldn't sleep and neither could Vanessa. The phone rang, and I answered it. Jay was on the line saying that they were at a rest stop. "Babe, I'll see you in about twelve hours."

"Jay, you may be too late. I feel like something's going to happen tonight." "OK!! I'll drive. What about if we make it in eight hours?"

"Jay, just come whenever you can get here, and don't speed." "Tell my son to hold on until I get there."

"I know you're wishing for a boy, but it may be a girl."

"You just tell Little Jay, I'll be there. Love ya. Bye." Jay really sounded excited about the baby, and I hoped it was a boy, for his sake.

May 10th at 12AM, I got up to go to the bathroom, and I saw a light on under the door of the front bedroom. Then I heard Daddy's voice. I knocked on the door and told Daddy that I needed to go to the hospital. Daddy said, OK, and everybody in the house got up to see me off. Mama called Dr. Jimson, so he could let the hospital know that I was coming. All the way to the hospital Daddy keep telling me to stay calm, not to get excited, and that everything was going to be alright. He was turning each corner on two wheels. We got to the hospital, and they were waiting for me. They took me right to the delivery room where Dr. Jimson was waiting, and twelve hours later, I had our son.

I went to sleep and woke up in the delivery room. The nurse told me that my parents were outside waiting to see me. She let them in. Mama was so excited, I could hardly understand what she was saying to me. I looked at Daddy, and he was so happy and excited that he was crying. (I hadn't even known that Daddy could cry.) Mama said that Daddy had already called Tallahassee, New York, and anybody that would listen, to tell them that we had a boy. I saw how much it meant to both of them for a boy to finally come into the family, and I thought that I'd name him Robert for Daddy. I thought, sorry Jay. He's your son, and he'll still carry your name, but just not Little Jay.

When they settled down, Mama asked me what I was going to name the baby, and I told her that his name was Robert. Mama screamed and Daddy cried again. They acted as if I'd given them my baby. I asked about Jay, and Mama said that she would call the house. Jay had made it in, and he was taking a shower, and he would be there as soon as he could. The nurse came back in. They wanted to take me to my regular room, so Mama and Daddy left.

The nurse took me to my room and told me that she'd bring the baby in in a couple of hours. I lay in bed, and I waited for Jay to come.

A wave of sadness came over me, and I got flashbacks of when I was in the hospital having the twins, and how Jay never came. I started to cry, and the more I cried, the angrier I got with Jay. I didn't care if he came or not; he was never there when he should be.

I turned over and tried to sleep again, but I heard Jay's voice outside my room. He came in and called me. I kept my eyes closed. Jay went around to the other side of the bed and kissed me, and I opened my eyes, but with no expression. I looked at Jay, and I knew that I loved my husband, but it was a bittersweet love, and the taste of disappointment still lingered. Jay bought me flowers, candy, and a matching, pink silk robe and gown. I said thanks and laid them on the table beside the bed and closed my eyes again.

"Louise!! Where's the baby? What's happened? What's wrong!?" "The baby's fine, Jay. They'll bring him in any minute now."

"YES!! I told you that you were going to have a boy, Little Jay. I can hardly wait to hold him. Call the nurse to bring him in."

"The nurse is bringing Robert in now." Jay's face was all lit up, and his eyes never left the baby as she gave him to me. I took him into my arms and held him close to my body. Then I counted his fingers and toes, and I thanked God for my son. I told Jay to come closer to the bed so that I could give him his son. Jay stood close to the bed, and he smiled as I gave him his baby boy, I said, "Jay, I'd like to introduce you to your son, ROBERT!"

Jay's face melted, his smile and the sparkle in his eyes were gone. He sat down and he held Robert, and talked to him, calling him Little Jay. He told him all the things they were going to do together. I told Jay to give me the baby so I could feed him. Jay stared out the window while I fed the baby. Then he walked back to the bed and held Robert's tiny little feet and told him that he'd always be his Little Jay. Still not talking to me, Jay stood there and watched me feed the baby. The nurse came in and said that it was time to go. Jay stood up, kissed me and the baby, and he left. I felt scared because I could see our marriage falling apart, and I was not even upset about it.

At 11 AM the next day, Mama and Bobbie came over to visit. They'd already stopped by the nursery to see the baby. They asked me how I felt, and I said, OK. Then they began talking to each other about who was going to keep my baby, and on which days. I didn't even bother to get in on the conversation. My mind was on Jay and me and our relationship and which way it was headed. The nurse came and said that they had to go because I had to feed the baby. Mama reminded me that she wouldn't be over the next day because I would be going home.

At 2 PM it was visiting hours again, and Joy was there with her friend Sam. She had a gift for me in a large, white box with a blue ribbon tied into a big bow. I opened the box, and it was a large, soft, blue blanket, tiny blue booties, a little blue outfit, and a tiny little cap that said, "Little Jay." I started to feel sad because I was already confused about my feelings for Jay, and I felt bad because he wanted the baby's name to be Jay Jr. I told Joy, Thank you, and that I was glad that they had come to see me. Joy's friend Sam couldn't sit still. He was looking out the door, out the window, he walked around the room, and he shook the change in his pocket. He was making me nervous. Finally Sam told Joy that he was ready to go. Joy came over to me and put the large white box with the baby things in it on the table for me and said good bye.

At 5:00 PM Jay walked into the room; he went over to the bed and gave me a kiss that felt almost as nice as the ones he used to plant on me. But maybe I was just not feeling Jay those days. He pulled the chair closer to the bed and sat down and said, "We need to talk. Babe, I'm sorry I left the way I did yesterday. I hope it didn't upset you."

"No, Jay, I'm fine." Jay was holding my hand and playing with the wedding band on my finger.

"When you told me that Little Jay's name was going to be Robert, it threw me a little, and I had to get a hold of myself, but I'm OK now." He's still calling Robert, Little Jay, I thought, will he ever get over that? Jay kissed my hand and told me to cheer up. He took a blue, velvet box from his pocket, opened it, and it was a gold, charm bracelet with two charms on it for May, because Vanessa and Robert were both born in May. Jay put the bracelet on my arm, gave me a kiss, and said, "HAPPY MOTHERS DAY." He had forgotten it the day before.

I said thanks, and I asked Jay what was going on in Detroit. "Babe, I want us to move back to Detroit. I've already started a business, and everything is moving along just fine. Once you're out of the hospital and can move around more, I want you to go up with me to look at a house in Cherry Lawn. If you don't like one there, we can look at some others."

"What kind of business is it Jay, and I hope Jim isn't involved in it." "Babe, why don't you like Jim, he thinks very highly of you."

"Well, you tell Jim, Thanks. But if your business involves Diamond Jim, I'm not going back to Detroit." The nurse brought the baby in just then and said that visiting hours were over.

"OK, Babe, we'll talk some more when I come and pick you up tomorrow." 1:00 PM the next day, the nurse had just come into my room, and I'd signed all of my discharge papers. I was waiting until Jay came to get Robert dressed. I thought that he would be pleased when he saw the little outfit that Joy had bought for Robert, and the little hat that said, "Little Jay." I heard Jay's loud voice down the hall even before he got to my room. He was telling the nurses to bring our son to the room so that we could leave. The nurses had already connected Robert to the father with the loud voice. They wheeled his little bed in and helped me dress him. The other nurse had a wheelchair ready to take me downstairs. Jay was telling everyone how good looking he and his son were, and the nurses were trying to get his loud mouth off of the floor. I sat in the chair, they gave me the baby, I waved good-bye to everyone, and we left.

We drove up in front of the house, and it looked like we were going to have a party. So many cars were parked out front; I wondered what was going on. Bobbie came out to the car and took Robert out of my arms so that I could get out. I reached for my baby, and she told me to go on into the house, and that she'd take him in for me. I got into the house, and everyone was there to see our baby boy and to tell Jay and me congratulations. Mama told Bobbie to take the baby in the room with me, because she didn't want everyone breathing on him. Mama told everyone to enjoy themselves, but they wouldn't see the baby anymore that day. She didn't want him in the room, because it was too soon for him to be around that many people.

Mama brought Vanessa in to see me, and she was all over me. She crawled into my arms and didn't want to leave. When everyone was gone and the kids were sleeping, Jay came in and told me that we needed to move. He had already found an apartment, and we'd move in two weeks. Jay said that we needed more privacy.

When June came, it was time to move. Jay came home, and we decided to tell Daddy at dinner. I told Daddy our plans, and Daddy said, OK, but Mama said it was too soon. I could see the tears filling up in her eyes, "Why don't you just leave Robert here with me, and see how you make out taking care of Vanessa by yourself." (Mama and Bobbie had taken over my baby from the day I had brought him home from the hospital.)

CHAPTER 33

Gone Again

Five months after we'd moved away from Mama's house, everything was fine. Jay had a new job managing a warehouse. Vanessa was walking, and Robert was eating everything in his reach. Then Jay came home, and he didn't talk to me. I wondered what was wrong. We ate dinner without saying a word to each other, and I had gotten tired of saying, "WHAT'S THE MATTER?" everytime Jay acted like that. So I didn't even acknowledge that he was in the room. I washed the dishes and went into the room to get the babies ready for bed. Jay came in to help. We put them to sleep. I showered and got into bed and read my magazine.

"Louise!"

"What!! You want to talk now?"

"Yeah, we need to talk about our business in Detroit. We'll need to make a move soon. Are you ready?"

"NO!! Jay you never told me what kind of business it is, or if Jim is involved in it."

"Well, that's why we're having this little talk now." "OK, so talk. What's going on?"

"Louise, the business is a supper club, and Jim is involved because we need his liquor license, because I can't get one."

"What is a Supper Club?"

"We'll serve dinner, have some music, and we'll also serve alcohol."

"No, Jay, let's just open up a restaurant."

"Fine time to think of that, after all the trouble I've been through."

Jay jumped up and packed his traveling bag again. He said he was going to Detroit. I asked him not to go. He said that I'd have the car, and he was leaving enough money for me until he got back.

"But what about your job, Jay?" He didn't answer. I sat around the room and pouted and pleaded for Jay not to go. Someone knocked on the door, and I knew it was Jim. I let Jay answer the door. He came back and put the keys and the money on the dresser, and then he wanted to kiss me. I pushed him away. Jay left out the door with Jim, and I cried all night.

I woke up the next morning, and I was sick as hell. I felt like I was pregnant again. I even got dizzy like I always did. But it couldn't be. I d been having my monthly, and it was never late. I thought that I'd call Mama and ask her to baby sit so I could see what was going on. I called Mama, and she said, OK, she'd take care of the babies while I went to see the doctor. I got them packed up and drove over.

When we got inside, Mama said, "You don't look so good, why are you going to the doctor?"

"I feel like crap."

Mama looked at me and smiled, "Well, if you're going to the doctor to see if you're pregnant, I could have told you that two months ago. You can save that money."

"But Mama, I'm still getting my monthly."

"I don't care, you're pregnant, and you can mark my word."

I wished Mama hadn't said that. Whenever Mama said, "Mark My Word," you were doomed, but I was going to the doctor anyway.

I went to see Dr. Jimson, and he told me that I was four months pregnant. I explained to him about my monthly, and he said that happened sometimes. He gave me vitamins and iron pills, and told me to come back the next month. During my drive back to Mama's house, I was thinking that this had to stop. I couldn't keep doing this, and now I was pregnant again, and Jay was gone again. I had to go through all that pain by myself. I had to stop having babies.

Mama never talked to me about sex, even after I got married. She never talked to me about what to do about getting pregnant. We would have to talk when I got to her house. I turned into the driveway, and I saw Bobbie's car. I should have known she'd be over there; whenever Robert was around, she was not far. I smiled and thought, Bobbie wants my little boy. When I got into the house, I didn't even have to tell Mama what the doctor had said. She just shook her head, and I confirmed it. Then she said, "You're pregnant!"

I said, "Yes." I told Mama that we had to talk about getting pregnant. She said, "You do know why you're getting pregnant, don't you?"

I looked at Bobbie and smiled, but I felt embarrassed because I've been pregnant twice already. This was my third, and now I finally wanted to talk about it. Mama never talked to us about sex, or getting pregnant, or what to do to keep from having so many babies. I asked Mama what I could do to keep from having all of these babies. Still in a joking mood she said, "Take an aspirin to bed with you."

"Take an aspirin to bed, why Mama?"

"When your husband gets into bed with you, put the aspirin between your knees and hold it there until he gets out of bed."

At first I didn't get it, because I was serious, but when Mama and Bobbie started laughing, I realized that Mama was playing. But at the same time Mama was telling something she had wanted to say to me early on—to keep my legs closed. But I was in no mood for jokes. I got the kids ready to go, and Mama told me what to do. She told me about the rhythm system. She said about two weeks before your monthly, and two weeks after, is the time you conceive—so don't sleep with your husband then. I was still confused. Mama said in our

185

religion, being Catholic, that we were not supposed to use anything to prevent us from conceiving. I said, OK, but I was still confused. I needed to talk to Dr. Jimson about this one, and in my confusion I got the babies ready to go.

Bobbie wanted Robert to spend the night with her. Bobbie loved Robert as if he was her baby. She would keep him forever If I'd let her. Mama said I should let Vanessa stay the night with her, because she knew I didn't feel good. I said, OK, and I left. I got home, and I lay across the bed, and I thought about the way Jay was treating me. How could he be so mean and cold? Everytime I was pregnant, he left me because something else was more important. And I didn't think it was business. I was going to find out just what it was.

The doorbell rang, and I opened the door. It was one of Jay's friends. I told him that Jay wasn't home, but he walked past me and went into the house. He took a seat and asked why Jay wasn't working at the warehouse anymore. Charles was a good friend of Jay's. They used to sit around on the weekend and watch football games and drink beer together.

"Charles, why are you asking about Jay's business? If he wanted you to know, he would have told you." Charles laughed, and I went into the kitchen to make some tea which I offered to him. He came into the kitchen, and he stood behind me.

"Yeah, I'll have some."

"You can go back in the living room, Charles; this kitchen is too small for both of us." Charles made sure he brushed against me as he left the kitchen. He turned around and asked for a mug. As I handed him the mug, he walked into me and brushed his arm across my breast. Alright, Charles, get out." I was thinking, I know this fool is not going to try anything with me.

"What's wrong with you Louise, what about my tea?" I pointed to the door, and I picked up the small pot of boiling hot water.

"Charles, get out now!" He smiled and walked to the door but not before telling me that Jay was the first and only man I'd made love to and that I should try sleeping with him, and I wouldn't miss Jay so much. I told Charles to go to hell. He laughed and closed the door. I was so angry I couldn't see straight. What had Jay been telling that man, and how much of our business did he know? Jay was to get into Detroit the next day, and I couldn't wait to talk to him.

The phone rang an hour later. I picked it up, and it was Charles. "Louise, please forgive me for what I said, I had too much to drink before I came over." I could smell the alcohol on his breath when he had been here, but Charles always smelled like alcohol.

"You had a few drinks, and you come into my home and disrespected me?" "No, Louise, I had a few drinks to get the nerve to tell you how I felt about you. I've wanted to be with you since the day we met. I really like you; I came over on the weekends so that I could be close to you. I was hopping that we could get together, but now that I know we can't, I won't be around anymore, even when Jay gets back. But if you get lonely, you know how to call me."

The more Charles talked, the more I wanted to throw up; the shit was getting deep. Who did he think he was talking to? I wasn't that naive. I was so shocked, I didn't even respond; I hung up the phone. That had been some day for me. I took a shower and got into bed, and I tried to read, but everything that had happened did a replay in my head: the pregnancy, the visit from Charles, and Jay gone. Every time I thought about Charles, I got mad. Yeah, he wouldn't be by anymore because he knew he'd messed up.

8AM the next morning Mama called to ask if Vanessa and Robert could stay until Sunday because Bobbie was going to pick her up, and they were going to buy them some little outfits for church. I said, Yes, because when I talked to Jay, I didn't know what kind of mood I was going to be in.

2 PM, the phone rang. "Hello"

"Hi, my name is Pauline, and I found your name and number in my husband's pants pocket."

"And who is your husband, Miss?" "Charles Abbott."

"Oh, yes, I know Charles; he's a good friend of my husband." "Well, why is your name on this note and not your husband's?"

"I don't know, Miss; you'll have to ask your husband." My goodness, first Charles, and then his wife! What else could happen to me? Pauline started to cry, and she told me everything that she and Charles had gone through. Pauline said that when they got married, Charles was tipping around on her before the ink was even dry on the marriage license. She said that she was the only one married in their relationship, not Charles. I guess Pauline just wanted to vent, she needed someone to talk to. I told her that I hoped things got better between them. I didn't have the heart to tell her what Charles had done the day before.

5PM, I made a long distance call to Detroit, and Jay answered the phone. He said that they had been there for an hour, and he was about to call me. Jay could tell by the sound of my voice that something was wrong. I let Jay know that I was pregnant, and that I had gone to the doctor the day after he left to confirm it.

And then I told him about Charles. "Jay, Charles came by the other day drunk as ever."

"Yeah, I told him that I would be out of town and to look in on you."

"He looked in on me alright, he even got fresh." I told Jay everything Charles had said to me, and he brushed it off.

"Babe, that's just the way he plays around. Don't even give Charles a second thought."

I even told Jay that I'd gotten a call from Pauline, and what she'd said about their marriage, but Jay said that Pauline was crazy. It was like a slap in the face. I couldn't believe that he'd taken everything so lightly. I asked Jay when he was coming back home. He said that he was returning to Miami to be with me during my pregnancy, but not right away. Jay said that he'd have to find someone to look after things while he was with me.

When Jay finally got back to Miami, I was almost in my seventh month. He had contacted Charles one month ago and offered him a job in Detroit with a generous salary. I couldn't believe it. This was the same man that had tried to seduce his wife, and Jay had offered him a job. But Charles got all the cheating and heartbreak thrown right back at him. I talked to Pauline that morning, and we talked about what happened to Charles.

Jay stayed in Miami until I had the baby, and Charles went to Detroit to run the Supper Club. He made good money and sent it home to Pauline. Then the money stopped coming, and Pauline began calling our house every week to find out what was going on with Charles. Jay called Detroit to find out what was going on with his friend, and he found out that Charles had gotten hooked up with Lisa—the same Lisa that Jim had taken from Opa-Locka to Detroit. Charles already had a drinking problem, and it wasn't hard for Lisa to get him hooked on cocaine. His drug problem got so bad that he couldn't open up The Club. He wasn't making the money he had made before. Because Charles got sick, he couldn't take care of all the things Lisa needed, and he couldn't take care of Lisa anymore. She sent him right back home to Pauline.

The lifestyle Charles had been living was too much for him. He returned to Miami and begged Pauline to take him back. Pauline loved Charles, and she gave him another chance to get it together. But it was too late for Charles. A month after they were back together, Charles died.

CHAPTER 34

Gone for Good

Jay and I had a terrible fight that morning, about going back to Detroit. I'd had my baby girl, Dee, but she came two months early. I didn't think that we needed to move yet. Jay thought I wanted to stay around my family. It was clear to me that Jay wanted to have his own way or else. Sometimes I thought that Jay was afraid of being a father and a husband. He always seemed to run out on us. Jay had stormed out of the house that morning. When he came back hours later, I could see the anger on his face, and I knew what was coming next. Jay had played that game many times, but it was going to be the last time. He thought I was going to wait for him to come back, when he was ready, but it wasn't going to happen, not this time.

Jay packed his bags, put money and the keys on the dresser, and I walked out of the room after he kissed the babies. When I walked out of that room, I walked out on us, our love and our marriage. Jay went into the living room where I was, and he just stood there. Then he reached out his arms to me, but I waved him away. He walked out the door, and I locked it. I hated Jay at that moment, and later I cried because I loved him. It had been a bitter/sweet love for a while then.

If I could have turned back the hands of time, Jay would be nowhere in the picture.

Two weeks later, I got a letter from Jay. He sent me money for the bills and for me and the babies. When I read the letter it said:

Hi Babe,

I haven't tried to call you because I know that you are still mad at me, and I knew that you would hang up on me or not even talk to me. But I want you to know that I love you. I know that I hurt you, and I'm sorry. Please forgive me. I want you to know that I've closed the Supper Club. When I had Charles helping me, he gave the place a bad name with the kind of people he had hanging around here. But I've opened up an After Hours Club in Lenny's Basement. After Hours Clubs are big up here. Everyone's doing it. I'll call you soon.

Love Ya!
Your Husband, Jay

When I looked at the letter, no matter what Jay said in it, all I could see was Jay still doing the same thing. He still didn't include me in his little world, and I felt rejected. He had sold the Supper Club and bought an After Hours Club without discussing any of it with me. He just told me how it was going to be, and that was it.

Ever since Jay left the last time, I had tried to imagine my life without him. Each time Jay left, it got harder to love him when he came back. Although Jay sent me money for the bills and a little for myself, I still needed to get back into nursing school and to get a job. I needed to find my own identity, other than being Jay's wife and the mother of his children. That wasn't enough for me anymore.

A month later, I had started attending a little technical school. I was training to become a nursing assistant, so that I could get a job right away. I would go back to nursing school after my babies were a little bigger. Since attending school, I had met Rick, an old classmate of mine. The first day I saw Rick, I didn't recognize him. He had become a mature, good-looking, young man. He didn't have that school-boy look anymore like he did when we were in high school. When we met, we shared a laugh about an old boyfriend of mine, Walter.

"Louise, remember your boyfriend Walter? He started a fight with me when you two broke up."

"Yes! I remember that, he got suspended for that, didn't he? Walter was a fool in those days. He said that you were trying to hit on me and that was why we were breaking up."

"Well, I need to make a confession, Walter was almost right."
"And what does that mean?"

"Maybe it wasn't the reason you broke it off with him, but I did try to hit on you, but you never took anything I said seriously."

"Oh, did you really!" I didn't know what to say, and I felt strange talking to Rick after he had said that he did try to hit on me. From the look in Rick's eyes, he still wanted to hit on me.

"Yeah! When I found out you were in love with some college guy, I gave it up."

"Oh, yeah, Jay. Look Rick, it's time for me to go back to class. Maybe I'll see you around sometime, bye." I left Rick standing there. He managed the whole sales TV shop in the building next to the school. I had a feeling that he would make sure that I got to see a lot of him. I didn't want to talk to Rick about Jay yet; I wasn't ready.

It was hard to remember how much I loved Jay then, and the way I felt about him currently. I didn't even tell him that I married Jay and had three kids with him. I used to be proud to be married to Jay, but now he was just a part of my past. There was a time when Jay's love had been all I needed to keep me satisfied. But I needed more from our relationship, and Jay was not giving it to me. I was glad that I wasn't addicted anymore.

Jay called me every week. He'd fill me in on what was going on at the After Hour that he was running. He wanted to know what was going on with the kids. When Jay called the night before, he said that he felt that something was wrong, and he wanted to know what the problem was. I said, Nothing. I didn't want to fight with Jay because I didn't care what he thought anymore. Just like the night before, each time I hung up the phone, I felt angry, betrayed, frustrated and confused. Then I'd remember the times when the sound of Jay's voice had excited me, and I'd know everything would be alright. But that wasn't the case anymore, and that made me sad because I was loosing my friend, my lover, and my husband.

It had been two months, and I was almost done with my training. The school had a job lined up for me, and I was to start the next week. Mama had really been there for me. She said that she'd baby sit for me, and of course, Bobbie would take Robert while I worked.

The last day of class, I couldn't get the car started after class. I had to get it fixed, as I needed it for work the next week. On my way to the pay phone to call Daddy to pick me up, Rick walked out of his building and into the parking lot. He'd parked about three cars down from my car. I told him that I couldn't get the car started, and he tried to help, but nothing worked. So Rick had my car towed to a garage, and he took me to Mama's house to pick up the kids, and then he took us home. When we got home, Rick helped me get the kids out of the car and into the house. I said, "Thanks," closed the door, and locked it. I watched him walk to his car and leave.

The phone rang, and it was Mama, "I just called to tell you to watch yourself with that man."

"Mama, he's just a friend. My car broke down, and I had to pick the kids up and get home."

"You could have called your daddy." "But Mama, Rick was already there."

"OK, I could see how that man was watching you. And I saw the way you smiled at him. You used to smile at Jay like that."

"Mama, we're just friends. OK?"

"You meet the same men over and over in life, the names and faces may change, but they will be the same person. Baby, don't start running from your past; you could wreck your future."

"OK, Mama, I'll remember that." What was Mama talking about? We weren't having an affair or anything. Were we? I wasn't really sure.

"I know you and Jay are having a rough time, but try to work things out with your husband. Getting tied up with that guy is nothing but trouble, MARK MY WORD now."

Oh, No! She said it again. I hated it when she said that.

Jay called that night. He seemed really excited about his After Hours Club. He said that business was good. When he was done rattling on about the business, I told him about the car. He said that I should find out how much it'd cost, and he'd send a money order for the mechanic. I called the next day, and I got the amount of the repair. Then I called Jay to let him know, and he said he'd send it to me. Later that evening, the mechanic drove the car up to my apartment building. Rick was leading him to the space with my apartment number on it. I could see Rick pointing to my apartment, and then he backed out and left. The mechanic came to my door and handed me a paid receipt. I didn't see Rick for about two weeks after that.

One day after work, I picked the kids up from Mama's, drove home, and when I turned into the parking lot, I saw Rick's smiling face. It pleased me to see him sitting there, just like it did when I used to see Jay. When Rick saw me, he hurried out of his car and walked over to help me get the kids out of the car. But first he gave me a slight peck on the cheek, and I gave him a soft rub on his back. When we got the kids all settled in, I went into the room and found the $119.00 money order that Jay had sent for the mechanic. I tried to give it to Rick, but he wouldn't hear of it. Rick said he had to go. He left me his phone number, and I found myself giving him mine.

The next day, Jay called as soon as I got in, and he was angry, because I wasn't home or at Mama's house when he called to talk to me. Mama just told Jay that I wasn't there. I had not told him about my nurse's training or my job yet. But since he was so upset about me not being at home, I had to tell him what I'd been doing. He didn't believe me. He accused me of having an affair, and I accused him of doing the same thing, and that it was the reason why he wasn't there with me and his three kids. What could be more important than his family? But Jay said that it wasn't true, and that he was coming home next week. I said, "Fine."

When I hung up, I thought, I'll have to call Rick and tell him not to call me anytime soon because the kids' father was coming home the next week. As I dialed Rick's number, I remembered what Mama had said. And even though we weren't actually having an affair, the possibilities were there. We just hadn't done anything about it. And I didn't want any trouble.

A week passed, and I expected Jay any day. I hadn't contacted Rick, and he hadn't called me. But I had been thinking about him a lot, and not my husband. I knew that was wrong, but I couldn't help it. When I thought about Jay coming back, my next thought was his rejection, and I felt betrayed because Jay Jay arrived home, and when we pulled into the parking lot, I saw him standing on the porch. Once Jay saw us, he smiled and ran down to the parking lot. When he got to the car, I had already started getting the kids out. Jay wanted to kiss me, but I put the baby into his arms. I could see that he didn't like my attitude.

"What's wrong with you, Louise?" "Nothing."

"Why are you being so cold?"

"I don't know what you're talking about."

"Yeah! I know something's wrong. When we get upstairs you're going to tell me what's going on."

"Jay, get that diaper bag out of the car for me please?" I asked him, trying to get his mind off of the subject until we got inside.

Jay was talking loud, and the kids were screaming, and I tried to get inside as fast as I could. Once we got inside, I fed the kids and gave them a bath. I tried to put them to sleep, but Jay woke them up. I could tell that it was going to be a long night, so I just let them stay up and play, cry, watch Jay act a fool, or whatever they wanted to do.

"Girl, what's going on with you?" "Nothing."

"Oh, so you're mad at me."

I got up and turned on the TV. I didn't even look in Jay's direction. He got up and turned the TV over—glass was all over the floor. "Jay, please stop acting so stupid."

"Stupid? I'll tell you who's stupid. That M— F— that thinks he's going to break up my family."

"Jay, no one's breaking up your family. You just can't keep it together." "Louise."

"What is it, Jay?"

"Do you still love me?" (Silence)

"Louise, Babe, please answer me. Do you love me?"

"Jay, you need to go to bed, so we all can get some sleep." "I guess the answer is No, huh?"

The kids were still screaming, and Jay was looking real crazy. Jay went into the bedroom and pulled out a small bottle of his Hennessey and tipped it up to his mouth, and when it came down his face looked like he'd just tasted bleach or something. I got up to call Daddy on the phone, and Jay ripped the phone from the wall. He told me to sit on the couch and not to move until he told me to. He put on some music, got a chair from the kitchen and put it in front of me, and sat down. Then he wanted me to pay attention to the record.

"Listen, Louise, do you hear what he's saying on the record?"

"Yes, I hear it, Jay."

"That man feels like I do. He said when a man loves a woman, he'll do anything she says." Jay was talking right in my face, and I wanted to gag. The liquor was so loud on his breath. He tipped the pint up again, and it was empty. Jay tried to be serious and confess his love for me, but Robert crawled onto my lap to get a good look at Jay while he was talking. When Jay tried to sing along with the record, Robert started to laugh. Vanessa had been hiding behind me, but she stood up and started clapping. When I laughed, Jay got mad and turned the music up louder, playing the same thing over and over again. As he tried to talk above the music, he told me that he wasn't going to give up on us. The loud music scared Robert and Vanessa, and they started crying again.

The building manager, Mr. Polk, called the police. When the police knocked on the door, Jay turned the music down. I was happy to see them when I opened the door. They walked in, and could see where Jay had knocked the TV over—it was still on the floor and there was glass everywhere. Then they saw the phone on the floor from when Jay had ripped it from the wall. The police told me that since Jay didn't put his hands on me, and since I wasn't the one that had called them, they couldn't do anything. So they were just going to take him down to the jail and let him sleep it off. I said, "OK."

The kids cried, and so did I. I needed some sleep because I had to go to work. I put the kids in the bed with me, and they all went right to sleep because they liked to cuddle up with me.

When I got up the next morning, the mess in the living room reminded me of the awful fight that we had. As I took the kids out to the car, I could see my neighbors watching me as I passed their apartments. I felt ashamed because of all the loud music, fussing and fighting that had gone on at our place the night before. It had been quiet around there until Jay came home.

When I got the kids to Mama's, she could tell that something was wrong. But I told her that I was running late, and I had to get to work. My day at work was terrible; everything I did was wrong. After work, I had a flat tire at the traffic light, and it was half an hour before anyone would help me. The cars would just pass or blow their horns for me to move out of the street. I finally got some help. And when I got to Mama's house, I had a fight with her about Jay. When I tried to tell her what had happened the night before, I found out that Jay had called Mama already and told her his side of the story.

Jay told Mama that I must be seeing someone else, because I didn't want anything to do with him. Mama said that we needed to try to work things out, and that I should get that other guy out of my system. I asked where my kids were, and Mama said that Bobbie had Robert and Dee, my baby, and I should let Vanessa stay with her because Jay and I needed time to ourselves. I didn't know about that, but I needed some time to sleep, so it was OK with me.

When I got home, I had to clean up all of the mess Jay had created the night before. Then there was a knock on the door, and it was the guy from Southern Bell Phone Company saying that he had an order to repair my phone line. Evidentially Jay had called the order in. While he was fixing the ripped out phone line, he noticed the phone was cracked too. Meanwhile, I took my busted, shattered, TV down to the dumpster. I got everything cleaned up, and I took a shower and made myself a sandwich. Then I got in bed to read a magazine.

It was 6:30 PM, and I knew Jay would come at any minute. I really didn't want him to come back, but I needed to get it over with. I had to let Jay know that I didn't want to be with him anymore. I didn't expect him to take it very well, but it was something I had to do.

I heard someone coming in the door, and it was Jay calling me as He walked through the door.

behind him, because I didn't want to fight again. "Are you sleeping?"

"Not anymore."

Jay came into the room and sat on the bed. He rubbed my leg and asked how I was feeling. I brushed his hand away, and I said, "I'm OK." I saw a flash of anger cross his face.

"Louise, can we talk?"

"Yeah, what's on your mind?"

"Please tell me the truth. Is there someone else?"

I folded my arms in front of me, and I answered, "No, Jay, there is no one else."

"Well, do you still love me?" "No."

"Why?" The look on his face, told me that I'd hurt him deeply. I wanted to take it all back, but I couldn't. I thought, I still love Jay; I just don't like him anymore.

"Jay, don't you know that every time you walked out on me and the kids, you left me frightened, confused and very unhappy. Now you've come back, and you're expecting everything to be the same? No, Jay! It's over."

"Babe, everything I did was out of loving you and to make things easier for you. All you had to do was stay home and take care of my kids."

The way Jay treated me sometimes made me think that I had traded "Daddy's Rules" for "Jay's Rules" and I didn't like it. "Jay, you wanted to have a family, and to live a single man's life at the same time. As much as you're gone, you could be living another life with another woman."

"Alright, maybe I didn't do things right before, but I do love you, and I'm sorry I made you feel bad. Let's just try to make it work. Give me a chance to do better. I'll make it up to you."

I wanted to forgive Jay, but I just couldn't. He had hurt me too many times. His time had run out; no more chances. We needed to go our own separate ways. "No, Jay, I don't think we can make it."

"Babe, you say that there is no one else in the picture, right? Then all you have to do is try to make it with me, one more time."

"I can't Jay, your love for me is too controlling. I need to be free from you." Jay was my first love; he had a spell over my mind.

"So you hate me now, huh?"

"No, Jay, I don't hate you. I just don't like you anymore."

At 12 AM, I told Jay, that by the end of the week, one of us had to go. Either he should leave, or the kids and I were going to live at Mama's. His bags were still packed and sitting in the corner anyway. Jay was like a visitor. I never knew how long it would be before he wanted to leave again. Jay went into the living room and played every love song he could find. And I got up and closed the door, but I could still hear the music play.

When Jay played, "La la Means I Love You," it made me think about the time through the music we listened to. That's how much we were in love and in tune with each other. The last song I heard before I went to sleep was, "My Girl."

2 AM, I woke up, and I felt something heavy pressing on my chest and on my body. I realized that it was Jay. I tried to push him away, but I couldn't. "Jay, why are you doing this?" He was already taking off my underwear, while I was sleeping.

"Babe, just relax. I just want to love you."

"Huh!" Did Jay say that he just wanted to love me? There was a time when I used to have sex confused with love, but not anymore. And this wouldn't change my mind. I let Jay make love to me until 3 AM. We slept until 7 AM. Then I got up, showered and got dressed for work, had my coffee, and took out something easy to cook for that night. Jay came into the kitchen with me as if everything was OK, because I had let him have his way the night before.

"Babe, I'm glad you changed your mind; you scared me for awhile there." "Who said that I changed my mind?"

"But what about last night?"

I walked into the bathroom to comb my hair and put on my make-up. "What about it?" I turned around and looked at Jay and waited for an answer.

"What we did last night. Didn't it mean anything to you?"

"No, Jay. And just for the record, that one was on the house, I didn't give it to you. You took it, and I just let you have it."

"I can't believe you're saying that, Louise."

"You know, Jay, I can't believe I said that either. But last night can't happen again. If you're not leaving, we're going to be staying at Mama's. Starting tonight, you and I can't stay here together."

When Jay moved out, he went to live at his mother's for a few weeks. Then he moved back to Detroit, where he ran an After Hours Club in his Uncle Lenny's basement. Ms. Lynn and Joy called me almost everyday trying very hard to somehow get us back together. When that didn't work, they called me everyday to tell me that I was a whore, a slut, and everything else they could think of. But I hung up the phone whenever I heard their voices. I knew Ms. Lynn didn't like me, but I never thought that Joy would turn on me the way she did. Mama had always told me that blood was thicker than water, and families should stick together no matter what.

After a few weeks, they'd blown off enough steam to stop calling. Sometimes when Jay would bring the kids back home, Joy or Ms. Lynn would ride with him to help with the baby, and they would speak to me, and I'd speak to them, just to be polite.

CHAPTER 35

A New Life and New Friends

It had been four years since Jay and I had separated. After we separated, he still spent a lot of time with the kids whenever he was back in Miami. He'd picked them up and keep them for the weekend, when there was nothing else going on in his life. He'd even pick them up on holidays.

One Easter Sunday Jay had spent most of the day with the kids. At about 4 o'clock Ms. Lynn called me to come pick the kids up. She said that Jay had been drinking a lot, and she didn't think it was safe for Jay to drive the kids across town. I said OK, I'd be there.

On the way to Ms. Lynn's house, I couldn't help but think of the times when Jay and I used to drive to Ms. Lynn's house the very route I was going. I thought about the talks we used to have, and the music we listened to. I even thought about how much I loved Jay back then. I never would have imagined us not being together.

As I pulled into Ms. Lynn's drive way I saw a lot of unfamiliar faces. I also saw my babies playing on the porch with their Easter baskets. I knocked on the door, and a lady that I've seen before opened it. I was still thinking, where had I seen her before?

My baby girl, Dee was trying to show me one of her toys. I picked her up and tried to introduce myself.

"Hi, I'm Louise."

"Oh, I know who you are, don't you remember me, I'm Debbie."

It was all coming back to me then, and it was the hair; she use to wear an afro. Now her hair was red with waves in it. I think, yeah! That's the Bitch everyone was trying to tell me about, when Jay had full control of The Club after Lenny had gotten sick. But I wouldn't believe a single word was true. I had faith in Jay, no matter what. "Jay wanted me to let him know when you got here," she said.

Debbie walked out to the backyard to get Jay, and I gathered the kids' toys and got them ready to go. Jay and Debbie came out of the house laughing and holding hands, and Ms. Lynn was walking behind them with the kids' diaper bag and a plate that she had wrapped for me. Jay and Debbie took the kids to the car, and Ms. Lynn handed me the plate of food.

"Hi Louise, how are you?" she said, but I wasn't speaking to her, I knew that she didn't care how I was doing.

Ms. Lynn put the plate down on the table, and I picked up my purse and Robert's truck and walked out the door, leaving that plate right on that table. When the screen door slammed shut, I heard Ms. Lynn say "That Bitch," and I laughed. When I got out to the car, I wanted to have a few words with both of them, but I didn't see the point.

Debbie went back into the house, and Jay was still standing there smiling, and he said, "I see that you've met my woman."

"Yeah, Jay, but this wasn't the first time I've met your woman. She's the same bitch you were staying out all night with at The Club when we were in Detroit."

Jay laughed and shook his head. "What are you talking? You know that The Club stayed open all night and we had to work. Anyway I don't owe you an explanation."

"No, Jay you don't, but I guess this is your way of letting me know what you were doing in Detroit, while I was down here having your babies." Jay laughed and called me a fool. He said that I was crazy, and that I was still in love with him.

"You're jealous, and you can't stand to see me with another woman. It's time for you to get on with your life."

I started up the car and pulled out, and I cried all the way home. The kids watched me, as I talked to myself about how Jay had cheated on me and betrayed me the whole time I trusted him. And then he sent for his woman, and he dangled their relationship in my face. And it did hurt for me to see them together. I needed to get on with my life. Jay was the only man I'd ever been with, ever, even since we've been separated. And although we weren't together anymore, I didn't know how to love anybody else, but I was ready to learn.

After I got home, I put the kids to bed. Then I couldn't stop thinking about Jay and Debbie, and how I had trusted them. But when I finally got to sleep, I dreamed that I was looking for Rick. I got up early the next morning, and I looked for Rick's number. I found it in my phone book.

I dialed Rick's number three times, and three times I hung up the phone. When I called that time, I was going to let it ring until he answered. Someone did answer the phone. The voice on the other end sounded smooth and sexy. I knew it'd been a long time since I'd talked to Rick, but I didn't remember him sounding like that.

"Hi Rick, do you know who this is?"

"No, but you sure sound like somebody I'd like to know, and by the way this is not Rick." The voice answered.

"Does Rick live there?" I asked.

now."

"I'm sorry, Sir, but my friend used to have this number." Rick must have moved since I'd talked to him over eight months ago. I wondered what had happened.

"No problem, is Rick a close friend of yours? Sorry I'm not who you want, and in case you're interested, my name is Jerry."

We laughed for a while and then I answered, "Hi Jerry, that was cute, but I haven't talked to him in over eight months now, I guess he'll have to contact me if he still wants to talk to me."

Jerry and I had talked for almost an hour before we knew it. I guess we both needed someone to talk to. Jerry asked if he could call me some time. I said, "Yes," and gave him my number. At least it'd be someone to talk to other than Mama. The kids kept me so busy, I never got out.

Jerry called me at least twice a week, for a month. Then we agreed to meet each other. I suggested a little Soul Food Restaurant near my job at 6 PM. As I drove to the restaurant, I thought to myself, I must be crazy meeting someone I'd only talked to on the phone. He could be a murderer or something. I wouldn't even know him if I saw him. I thought, I should have asked him what he was going to wear, but it was too late then.

As I walked in, I saw four guys, but they all had dates. So I just took a booth where I could see everyone that came in. I wished that Jerry had come early, it was almost six then. A few customers had walked in; two guys standing at the door seemed to be looking for somebody. Then they started walking my way. Maybe they worked together, I thought. But the white guy that was with the brother sure looked good: tall, cute, and he had nice brown cropped hair.

He slide into my booth and smiled again. "Are you waiting for Jerry?" He asked.

"Yeah, what happened, where is he?" "He's sitting right here with you."

"You're Jerry?" I almost choked; I didn't know what to say. Until I met Jerry, I'd always thought I'd know if a guy was white or black by the sound of his voice on the phone. But I guess I was wrong. When I looked at Jerry's beautiful, brown eyes, I got lost in them, and his smile showed off the dimple in his left cheek. The waitress came over to our table, and we ordered some drinks, red wine for me and a Miller for Jerry. We talked and laughed while we waited for our dinner.

After we finished eating, I had another glass of wine, and Jerry had two more Millers. They played music the whole time we were eating, and Jerry seemed to know a few of the songs that were playing. After Jerry finished his last Miller, he started to sing the song that was playing, "Going in Circles," and his voice was as smooth as velvet. I told him how much I loved his voice, and he told me about the music collection he had at home. I'd never gone out with a white guy before, but I could tell that Jerry had never dated a black girl before either.

When the evening ended, I'd agreed to go with Jerry to his apartment to listen to some of his albums. I followed him in my car. When we got to Jerry's apartment, he put on some music while I relaxed on the couch. Jerry brought me a tall glass of wine and sat down on the couch next to me. He kissed me, and it felt good. And then I was thinking, damn!! Jerry had it going on; I could get used to this. But I had to admit though, my curiosity was the reason things got that far with Jerry, because Jay was the only one I'd ever kissed. I could only measure Jerry's kiss by the kisses I had had with Jay. So at that point, it wasn't about a white or black kiss to me. It was about a kiss from another man, and how I felt about being intimate with him. Jerry was curious too; he kissed me again and again until I pushed him away. I told Jerry that things were going too fast. I don't think that Jerry was ready to stop, but he did. He walked me to my car, and he made me promise him another date. I said, "OK."

CHAPTER 36

Jay's Jealousy

When I left Jerry's, I went by Mama's to get the kids. I got inside, and Mama had a phone number for me. It was a note with Rick's name on it, and a message saying that he had been transferred out of town with his job. There was also an address for where Rick lived.

As I took the kids out to the car, I was excited, and I was thinking that things were looking up for me. I would wait until the next day, after I got off work, before I would call him. As soon as I got home, the phone rang. I picked it up, and it was Anne. She told me that Al wanted her to take him back. And I warned Anne to think about what she was doing first. But that wasn't the reason that Anne had called. She wanted to let me know that she had seen Rick. "Oh! Yeah," she said, "I saw Rick yesterday. You never told us that Rick had kids."

"What are you talking about?" I asked.

Anne said that while she was at the store, she saw Rick, and he had a little boy with him. She said when they got out of the car, she was going to her car. Rick remembered Anne—they had met at Mama's when Rick took me home once. Rick spoke to Anne. He said that the little boy was his son, and his name was Tim. They were going into the store to pick up the little boy's mother, because she worked there.

Rick also told Anne that he had a little girl, but she didn't live there, and she had a different mother too. But if I know my sister, Rick didn't just volunteer all of that information. Anne had a way of getting all kinds of information out of anyone. Her husband, Al, got the third degree all the time; it was no wonder he drank the way he did. Once I got Anne off of the phone, I went right to bed and slept until morning. Then I thought about Rick all day until I got off from work.

It was 3 pm when I picked the kids up. I'd had a good day at work, and I thought that I would do everything I had to before I called Rick. That way there wouldn't be any noise in the background while we talked. I didn't even know what I was going to say. It had been such a long time since we'd talked. I was glad he hadn't forgotten me.

At 4:30 PM, I walked into the house, and I could hear Vanessa and Dee playing on the porch. "Hi Mama, how were the kids today?"

"They are OK, but Bobbie has your son. She picked him up an hour ago." "I thought once Bobbie had her daughter, she'd get over my son."

"I think Bobbie really wanted a son." "I think you're right."

I wanted to tell you last night, before you took off, that Anne said that she saw Rick at the store."

"Yeah, Mama, I know. She called me last night and told me everything." "Everything?"

"Yeah, Mama, everything."

"OK, I see you don't want to talk about it." "We'll talk about it later, Ma. Got to go, love ya!"

I got Dee and Vanessa into the car and took them home. I fed them and bathed them, and we had our little playtime. My mind was on what I was going to say to Rick when I called him that night.

At 9:30 PM I rang Rick's phone for the second time; he must have still been out. While the phone was ringing, I thought about Jerry. He had Rick's old phone number. The last time I had tried to call Rick, I had ended up having a very nice conversation with Jerry. I would never forget him. I dialed Rick's phone number again.

"Hello."

"Hi Rick, it's Louise."

"Hey, I was just thinking about you." "So what's going on?"

"Well, first of all, let's talk about your sister. I know she told you what happened."

"Yeah, Rick, she did. But why didn't you ever tell me about your kids?" "Because I didn't know at the time if you needed to know."

"And what does that mean?"

"It means that once I found out about Jay, you never told me about your kids, until I happened to take you to your mother's house to pick them up. Remember that day?"

I knew exactly where Rick was going with this, and the bottom line was, "The pot can't talk about the kettle," as Mama always said. "OK, OK, Rick, I get it. You didn't know where our relationship was going. And before we ever got any closer, I called you that night and told you that Jay was coming back and not to call or come by."

"Yeah, that's true, but I still wanted to be with you, no matter what." "OK. So tell me about your kids?"

"Well, you may know my son's mother. You remember Pam? She was in our English class. She was also my prom date. Pam and your friend Sandy used to fight all the time."

"OH! Yeah, I remember Pam. She was pregnant at graduation." "But I didn't know, she never said anything to me."

"When did you find out?"

"Right after graduation, my mother sent me to D.C. with her brother, so that I could work in his shop. Three months after I was there, I met a young lady by the name of Marsha. She was pregnant by me, and we were going to get married. I wrote home and told my mother, and she told her friends that I was getting married. Pam lived on the next street, and when she heard about me getting married, she finally told her mother that I was the father of her baby.

"Did you still get married?"

"No. My mother called D.C. to let me know about Pam, and my cousin told Marsha, and she and her family didn't want anything to do with me then. Her mother called the wedding off, but Marsha had another kid. She just got married last year. So there you have it. Are you still talking to me?"

I said yes, I was still talking to him. I told him what was going on with Jay and me and the divorce. We must have talked for at least three hours. By the end of the night, we'd made plans for a date on the weekend.

5 PM the next day, Jay called me at work. He was pissed off because he had been served with divorce papers. I didn't know why Jay was so mad; it's not like the divorce was a surprise. He had even told me to move on with my life. And I was doing just that. Jay wanted to come over to my place that night to talk. But I had already promised myself that after the night he broke the TV and pulled the phone from the wall, I'd never be alone with Jay again. I told him to meet me at Mama's house at 5 PM. He agreed to meet me there.

It was 7 PM, and Jay still hadn't showed up at Mama's. I gathered the kids' things, thanked Mama, and we got in the car and went home. Once I got the kids settled in, I was going to bed. If Jay wanted to talk, he could call me the next day.

At 9:39 PM, someone knocked on the door. I looked out the window, and my heart dropped. It was Jay. I opened the door to let him in, and he went into my room where the kids were. He fell on the bed, and the kids were all over him.

I went into the room where they were playing. I stood by the bed and folded my arms, and I asked, "Jay, why are you here?"

"I told you I needed to talk to you."

"And I told you to meet me at Mama's house. But you are here now, so what did you want to talk about?"

"I want to talk about this divorce. I thought that we would have gotten back together before this shit got this far."

"Now, let me see. So you were thinking of getting back together with me so we could raise our kids together. But you sent for that bitch to come from Detroit and to stay there in your mother's house with you. And then you told me to get on with my life. Boy, you need help.

"Louise, I'll tell you what, if we get divorced, I'm going back to Detroit when Debbie leaves, and I won't be back until they send me a court date. You've got a week to think about it.

"And I'll tell you what! You didn't have to come back the last time. And you can leave tomorrow, I still don't want you."

I thought about what Jay had said, and I wished it was that simple. But things could never go back to the way they used to be. At least not for me. But Jay didn't even acknowledge my anger. He reached for my hand to hold it, but I pulled it back. Jay looked at me and smiled.

"Louise, it hasn't been that long. We used to break up and then turn around and make up, and you enjoyed it. Remember?"

Jay was right. Every time I heard his voice, and he said that he was sorry, my heart melted and I forgave him. But his magic spells lost their touch long ago. Jay flopped on the bed, and he pulled me down with him. He tried to play around, but I didn't want to, and I told him to go home. Jay told me to stop acting like a bitch.

Once Jay realized that there was no use trying to get on my good side or even talking to me, he got angry and started to talk loud until he woke Dee up. She started to cry. When I went to her bed to get her, Jay took Vanessa and Robert out of the house. When I realized what was happening, they were already getting into the car. When Jay backed out, he told me that he wasn't going to bring them back.

He left me standing in the middle of the parking lot screaming, "JAY BRING THEM BACK." Everyone that lived in the building watched me stand there holding Dee and crying and calling for Vanessa and Robert.

I went inside and called the police, but I got no where with them because Jay was their father. I called Mama, and I told her what happened. Mama told me to calm down. She said he would bring them back. But I didn't want to hear that. I wanted her and Daddy to ride out to Ms. Lynn's house with me, so that Daddy could kick Jay's ass, and Mama and I could beat the hell out of Debbie and Ms. Lynn. But they didn't, and I hung up the phone.

But they were at my door within ten minuets. I let them in, and we all sat down. Mama said that no matter what Jay had done, even before we had this fight, she believed that Jay really loved me, and he wanted to come back. I didn't want to hear anything about how much Jay loved me, because I hated him then.

"But Mama, what about my kids? They don't know Debbie."

"Louise, Jay won't let that woman hurt those kids."

"They might try to take them back to Detroit. I might never get my children back." I started to cry again. Mama made me stand up while she talked to me. She told me to pay attention to what she was saying.

"When that woman sees those howlin' children, she may send them back tonight. And if not tonight, give them a couple of days. Debbie doesn't want those kids; she wants Jay. Think about it, Louise. That woman wants your husband, and she needs no distractions. If she can't get Jay's attention, she can forget it. And having your kids around won't help matters any.

Mama almost made me want to take Jay back, just to keep Debbie from being with him. But it didn't take long, before I snapped back and remembered that Jay was no good for me.

After two days, Jay still hadn't brought the kids back. I'd been talking to Mama and Anne, every day, and they said that I should go on my date with Rick as planned. But I was still worried about the kids, but I was also excited about my date that night.

At 6 PM I heard Rick knocking. I opened the door for him, and the phone rang. I waved Rick into the house and ran to the phone. When I answered the phone, no one answered. I hung up, but I had the feeling that it was Jay. I got my purse and we walked out to Rick's car. He started the car, and I turned on the radio. Then Rick leaned back, looked at me, and told me how nice I looked. I said, thank you. Rick kissed me, and it took my breath away. There was something really special about Rick's kiss. I didn't know what it was, but I liked it. After I caught my breath, I tried turning the radio to another station, and Rick backed out and drove to the Diner.

Once we got to the restaurant, we sat in the car in front of the diner, and we talked about how we were going to end our evening. As we talked, I could see Jay's car pull up at the Dairy Queen, and he and Debbie got out of the car. They had Robert and Vanessa, crying there little eyes out, with them. Jay took them by the hand and sat them on a bench in front of the Dairy Queen. I wanted to run over and grab my babies and put them in Rick's car and drive off. But Rick made me realize that my plan would both confuse the kids and put them in danger.

We tried to get out of the car without letting the kids see us. But when I closed my door, Debbie looked our way. I could see her telling Jay that we were across the parking lot. They stood in front of the kids to keep them from seeing us, while we went in. I was glad, because if they had seen us and stared to cry, there would have been a fight, and I would have taken my kids from them.

As I walked in, I looked at Jay and his eyes were on fire. I couldn't hear what Debbie was saying, but she was talking and giving Jay pure hell. I was glad that I had kept my date with Rick, and after Jay saw us,

I felt better. I know that Jay wanted me to be miserable without him, but then he saw that I was moving on too. The waitress came over and took Rick and me to a nice seat in the corner, and we had a tall glass of wine and some good conversation. Then we had dinner.

After dinner, we went into the back of the diner where they had a lounge. We listened to some music and danced. When we got ready to leave, I realized that it had been four hours since I'd seen my kids crying. But I was sure that I'd have them back the next day. After that night, Jay should realize that he didn't make me as miserable as he would have liked to. We got into Rick's car, and we drove back to my place. Rick drove into the parking lot of my building, and Jay was parked next to my car.

I told Rick to pull off and leave Jay there, but Rick refused to. He also reminded me that we hadn't done anything wrong. Jay and I had been separated for awhile then, and Jay was living with someone. So why should we run or feel guilty? Rick's words gave me strength to stand up to Jay. I watched Jay sit in his car and look at me. Rick got of the car, and he walked around to my door and opened it.

CHAPTER 37

What Ever Happened to Mr. Polk?

When I got out, Jay opened his door and got out. As we walked to my apartment, Jay followed us. The manager of my building told me that he'd been watching Jay sit in the car for three hours, and he had called the police when he saw us drive up. Jay heard him and turned around to get back into his car, but the police were already there. They talked to Jay, and the manager told me again that I had to move, because my situation was causing too many problems.

I was very upset, and Rick came inside with me and tried to comfort me. He put some music on and found his way around in the kitchen and got a tall, cold glass of wine for me. While Rick was in the kitchen, I thought about Jay. He wanted it all. He was with Debbie, but he wanted to keep me hanging on. Rick brought in the drinks and sat them on the table. Then he sat next to me and put his arms around me and told me to dry my eyes—that there was no need for me to cry anymore. He said he'd always be there for me.

I started to feel relaxed, and Rick kissed me. We agreed not to let Jay spoil the night for us. I lay on the couch while Rick entertained me with the music and showered me with hugs and kisses. We ended the night in each others' arms.

Saturday morning at 9 AM, the phone was ringing off the hook. I picked it up, and Jay was on the other end talking as loud as his voice would let him. And I heard Debbie crying in the background. She was telling Jay that she was leaving him, but he didn't hear her because he was fussing at me.

"I know that you had that M— F— in my bed last night, he was still there at 5 AM this morning."

"Jay, were you watching my apartment all night?"

"So what if I did, but he'd better not be there when I get there. And you can tell that li'l fat M— F— not to get in my way, if you want me to bring these kids back."

"Who are you talking about Jay, what fat M— F—?" "Your building manager, that's who."

Jay had no idea that that li'l fat M— F— wanted me to get out of there in two weeks, and it was all because of him. But I wasn't going to tell Jay about it, I just wanted my kids back right then.

"OK, Jay, just bring the kids."

"That other M— F— better be gone too." I hung up the phone and told Rick to leave because Jay was bringing the kids home.

"OK, Louise, I see how upset you are, so I'll leave, and I'll call you later about the move."

"OK, Rick, thanks for understanding." Rick gave me a kiss and left.

At 12 PM Jay and the kids were knocking on the door. I opened the door and I was so happy to see them I almost forgot how angry I was with Jay. They were still crying, and they were each trying to get my attention as Jay looked on. Then he told them to go to their room so we could talk. He closed the door to the bedroom, and someone knocked on the front door. I opened the door, and it was Mr. Polk, our building manager.

"Are you OK, Ms. Louise?" "Yes, Mr. Polk, I'm OK."

"Don't forget what I told you. Two weeks." Why did he have to say that? Two weeks. I didn't want Jay to know that I had to move in two weeks, even though it was all because of him. Mr. Polk turned around to leave, and Jay opened the door and slammed it shut.

"What about 'two weeks,' what is Fat Boy talking about?" "The rent is going up in two weeks; you going to pay it?"

"I know you're not being straight with me, and Fat Boy doesn't want me around because he wants to get to you. When he gets me out, he'll still have to worry about that other M— F—."

"Jay, that's a lie, and you know it."

All I wanted to do was think about Rick and me and our night together, and Jay was making the whole night seem awful.

"Babe, all I want to do is keep my family together, and you keep pulling away."

"Did you say that you want to keep your family together?" "Yeah!"

"Then why would you send for Debbie to come and stay with you?"

"Don't worry about Debbie, that bitch is crazy. I took her to the airport this morning. She's back in Detroit."

"You called me a fool at your mama's house last week, and now you say that Debbie's crazy. You've got problems, My Man."

Jay didn't even care about what I was saying. His mind was set on us getting back together, but he didn't really love me. I wished he'd just let me have somebody else.

"Look, I'm sorry for what I said, but I'm not giving up on us." "Why don't you get out of my life and let me have somebody else?"

"NEVER!" Jay got up, walked out and slammed the door. I didn't hear from him for two days. Maybe Jay did love me, but he was too controlling. I couldn't spend the rest of my life being Jay's lover and his kid too.

At 5 PM, I was on my way to get my baby. It'd been a week since Robert and Vanessa had seen her. I didn't know how I was going to tell

Mama that I had to move in two weeks and why. When I got inside, I could tell that Jay had already been there to tell his side of the story. Mama was standing in the dining room doorway, with her hands on her hips, and her mouth tucked in, shaking her head.

"OK, Mama, what did Jay say? I know he's been here spreading lies."

"Jay said that you're carrying on with two men over there. He said that you're sleeping with some man you had over there last night and Fat Boy. Now who is Fat Boy, and how does he know you had a date with Rick last night? Louise, what is going on?"

"Mama, when Rick took me home after our date last night, Jay was in the parking lot—he'd been there for three hours before we got back. Mr. Polk saw him and called the police; they made him leave. And Jay watched my apartment until 5 am this morning. And now I have to move because of Jay."

"Jay didn't say anything about you having to move."

"I didn't tell Jay because I don't want him to know. Mr. Polk told me I had to move while the police were talking to Jay."

"Why do you have to move, and why won't you tell Jay?"

"Mr. Polk said that last night was the third time the police had to come to my residence, and that was the limit. So I have to move."

"So what are you going to do?" Mama asked. "I don't know."

"That Boy says he wants to take ya'll back to Detroit." Daddy said.

"I'm not going back to Detroit. I've already told Jay, 'I'm Not Going Back.'" Everyone was standing around looking at me. I could see Claire and Kay looking so serious, and I knew what they were thinking—they were hoping that we wouldn't have to move back home. I remembered what it was like when Anne and her family lived with us in the old house.

"Cheer up, Claire; we won't be moving in here, OK?" And I heard a sigh, and I saw a smile that said, Thank you.

I packed up Dee's bag, picked her up, and we left. I had to call Rick when I got back home. I thanked Mama, and we left.

On my way back home I start thinking about all that had happened to me, and I just felt like giving up. I could feel my eyes fill up with tears, and I just couldn't hold them back. As the tears ran down each side of my face, I thought about how Jay had gone to Mama and told her such lies about me. Why wouldn't he just let me get on with my life, and let me live again, without him?

By the time I drove into the parking lot, the kids were watching me. Vanessa offered me one of her toys, and Robert asked me to please stop crying. I parked the car, and we all got out of the car and walked through the parking lot to the building. Just as we got to our apartment, Mr. Polk came out of his apartment to let me know that Rick had come by.

"Louise, your visitor from last night came by." "Oh! Did Rick leave a message?"

"No, I didn't talk to him. When I heard him knocking on the door, I looked out to see who it was." Mr. Polk seemed a little too concerned about my business; he even looked annoyed that Rick was there. I was glad that I'd be leaving in two weeks, maybe sooner.

"Thank you, Mr. Polk."

"Looks like you've been crying; what's wrong?" "I'm OK."

"I hope I'm not a part of your troubles. If you get rid of some of your visitors, I'll let you stay—you know what I'm saying?"

I opened my door and waved the kids in, and I sat Dee on the couch. I came back to the door for the diaper bag that I'd set by the door, and Mr. Polk was still standing there. He picked up the bag and handed it to me. When I took the bag, he squeezed my hand and told me to think about what he'd said. I was disappointed with Mr. Polk; I'd always considered him a good manager who was concerned about my safety. But he wanted to do exactly what Jay had accused him of doing. I had to get out of there; I never wanted to look in Mr. Polk's face again.

Once I closed the door, I wanted to call Rick right away, but I was still shaking from talking to Mr. Polk. He was as old as Daddy! How could he want to get with me? It was disgusting.

At 7 PM, the kids were settled down, and I was more relaxed. I thought that I'd call Rick.

"Rick?"

"Yeah, I came by earlier, but you were out." "Mr. Polk told me that you were here." "That's a strange dude."

"I know he is, and after I talked to him today, I'm afraid of him." I told Rick what Mr. Polk had said and how he'd squeezed my hand. Rick said that he was coming right over.

"Need to come over so I can kick Fat Boy's ass," Rick blurted out angrily. "Please Rick, don't come over. It'll be trouble for me."

"Louise, you can come here with your kids whenever you're ready to."

"Rick, let me think about it." I didn't want to move in with Rick because we'd just gotten into a relationship, and besides that I needed time to myself.

"OK, whatever you say. Oh yeah, what happened this morning when Jay brought your kids back?"

"He wants us to get back together."

"I knew he was going to do that, and what did he say about the woman we saw him with at the Dairy Queen last night?"

"They had a fight, and he took her to the airport this morning." "Looks like Jay's been busy today."

"More than you think; Jay went to Mama's house and told her that I was sleeping with you and "Fat Boy," as if he knew it for a fact."

"That boy's got troubles. He watched your apartment until 5 AM, went home and had a fight with his woman, sent her back to Detroit, tried to get you and your kids back, and then went and told your mama who he thinks you're sleeping with."

"I hope that Jay doesn't give me anymore trouble today."

"I'm coming over in about twenty minutes; you won't have any trouble out of Jay or Fat Boy. Something's got to be done about Fat Boy. Somebody's going to have to shut him up." Rick hung up the phone, and I went into the kids' room to make sure they were OK while I waited for Rick to come over. As I sat on the floor with Robert and Vanessa, I could hear a lot of noise at my front door. When I went out to see what was going on, I saw Jay and Mr. Polk arguing.

"You have to leave right now, Buddy. I don't want no trouble over here tonight," Mr. Polk told Jay.

"Who the hell are you calling Buddy, Fat Boy? Get out of my face."

"I'll have the police run you in this time."

"Go ahead, Fat Boy; I see you're going to have to be dealt with."

I opened the door, and Jay came inside, and Mr. Polk went into his apartment to call the police.

"What happened, Jay?" I already knew why Mr. Polk was badgering Jay, but I didn't say anything.

Jay came in and sat down. He asked me if I would sit down and talk with him again. I said, OK, and I hoped that he'd get on with what he had to say.

"Babe, I don't have much time to talk because Fat Boy said he's calling the cops for me, and I don't want to cause you anymore trouble. I really want you and the kids to come to Detroit with me. My After Hours Club is doing very good. I'm having someone taking care of everything for me now, but I need to be there handling things myself. Take this money, and you and the kids come on up to be with me. Please, Louise, I want you to be with me. Jay got up and walked out of the door. I went to the window and watched him get into his car.

As he was pulling out, the police were coming in with their lights flashing. I moved away from the window and closed my curtains. I went into my room with the money that Jay had given me and counted it. There was seven thousand dollars there, and I had no intention of going to Detroit. If Jay thought that the cash would buy me back, then he was a fool. I took the money and put it in a box on the top shelf of my closet.

Someone knocked on the door, and I already knew that it was Rick. When I opened the door for Rick, he asked me what had happened, and why the police were next door talking to Fat Boy. I told Rick, and he said that somebody was going to hurt Fat Boy.

Rick and I sat on the couch and talked and played around while we listened to some music. Later Rick went out and got some Chinese food, some red wine for me and some beer for himself. When he got back, he brought in the food and the drinks and told me to hold the door open, Rick opened his trunk and got a TV out and brought it inside. Fat Boy stood on the porch and watched him.

"Louise, what time does Fat Boy go to sleep, or does he watch your apartment all night?" Rick made sure that he said it loud enough for Mr. Polk to hear him.

I replied loudly, "Is Mr. Polk still out there?" Rick and I laughed, and Mr.

Polk slammed his door.

Rick and I ate, watched TV, and shared another night together. I realized that I could never go back to Jay. I was falling for Rick.

A week passed, and I talked to Rick everyday after I picked up the kids and came home. I get a phone call from Jay one night, and he wanted to know when I and the kids were going to join him in Detroit.

"Hi Babe, let me know when you're going to fly up, so I'll know when to pick you up from the airport."

"Jay, you know I'm not going to Detroit, so don't try to act like you are just waiting for me."

"Why didn't you tell me you weren't coming when I was there?"

"I never told you that I was coming either, and you walked out when you gave me the money anyway."

"You got the money—now you're talking shit, huh!?"

"Seven thousand dollars is nothing, Jay. When we got the money from our daughter's death, you did what you wanted to do with it, and I never said a word about it. You had your Supper Club and now your After Hours Club, and what did I ever get out of it? Nothing. I've been cheated; you owe me more than seven thousand dollars."

"What about the car? I bought you a car."

"No, Jay, you bought yourself a car, and you let me drive it while you were out of town. Remember I was pregnant most of the time you were out of town, and I had to get to the doctor some how."

"Alright, OK, just keep the damn money. I don't want to hear all of that shit, but will you just come to visit me?" Someone knocked on the door, and I told Jay to hold on. I opened the door, and it was the police again, and I wondered what Fat Boy had called them for this time. The officer said that Mr. Polk had been missing for a week, and they wanted to question me. I told them to come in, that someone was on the phone, and I needed to hang up. Jay had already heard what was going on; he said he'd call back.

"When was the last time you saw Mr. Polk?" The officer asked. "I saw him twice on Sunday."

"Did you talk to him?" "No."

"What was he doing when you saw him?" "He was talking to my ex-husband." "What were they talking about?"

"He told Jay not to come over anymore because he always started trouble." Another police officer came in and was telling the first officer that one of the ladies up stairs ex-boyfriend had a run-in with Mr.

Polk three months ago. She said that Mr. Polk was strange; he didn't like it when her boyfriend visited too often.

"What kind of trouble did your Ex cause?"

"We were separated, but sometimes when he came over, we had fights about the kids or he'd want to come back to me, and he'd get really loud, and Mr. Polk would call the police."

"When was the last time you saw Mr. Polk?"

"When my friend Rick came over and brought in a TV from his car. Mr. Polk was standing on the porch."

"Give me your friend and your Ex's name and how they can be reached, and thank you for your time."

We learned later that Mr. Polk had been tied up, beat, and left for dead in the back of the building, in one of the utility rooms. When they took Mr. Polk to the hospital, he stayed in a comma for three weeks. But when he came out of it, he didn't know anyone, and he couldn't talk anymore. The last I heard, they had to put Mr. Polk in a nursing home. The police questioned everyone, but they never found out who assaulted Mr. Polk.

Whenever I talked to Rick or Jay about it, they both laughed and said that Fat Boy had it coming to him, but they both said that they didn't do it.

Two and a half years after Mr. Polk was assaulted, I was still living in my same had to move, and there was no one to tell me that I had to get out then.

Jay and I were divorced by then, and he lived in Detroit. When he came to Miami, he visited the kids and sometimes he took them to visit Ms. Lynn. Since our divorce I've come to realize that Jay does love his kids. He just didn't know how to be a father and take care of a family, since his family was so dysfunctional. But that's something Jay will have to work out for himself.

As for me, I know who I am, and what I want now—thanks to the people I've met and the experiences I've had.

The last time I saw Jerry was at the Diner on Seventh Avenue. I was with Rick, and Jerry was with some blonde. They were sitting at the table next to us. When our eyes finally met, we shared a smile and a moment that was puzzling to Rick and Blondie.

Sandy and Sid got a divorce, and she's still tipping around with Ben.

Anne and Al divorced; Al went back to Tallahassee, and Anne got married again.

Joy went back to school and graduated, and then she moved to L.A. with her aunt.

Bobbie and Freddy finally had the son that she always wanted. They bought a beautiful home in Broward County and are very happy.

Although Rick and I never moved in together, we still loved each other. We had a baby daughter, Chekena, together, and we love her very much. I want to take full control of my own life now, and I hope that Rick really understands that. Since my divorce from Jay, I feel free, and I want to feel that way for awhile. I want love that requires no demands, and no expectations. With time, maybe I'll find it with Rick.

www.ingramcontent.com/pod-product-compliance
Lightning Source LLC
Chambersburg PA
CBHW030924120626
46554CB00001B/264